Better Homes and Gardens.

COOKIES

First Edition. First Printing.
Library of Congress Catalog Card Number: 86-62162
ISBN: 0-696-02201-X

BETTER HOMES AND GARDENS® BOOKS

Editor Gerald M. Knox
Art Director Ernest Shelton
Managing Editor David A. Kirchner
Copy and Production Editors James D. Blume, Marsha Jahns, Rosanne Weber Mattson, Mary Helen Schiltz

Food and Nutrition Editor Nancy Byal
Department Head, Cook Books Sharyl Heiken
Associate Department Heads Sandra Granseth, Rosemary C. Hutchinson, Elizabeth Woolever
Senior Food Editors Julia Malloy, Marcia Stanley, Joyce Trollope
Associate Food Editors Linda Henry, Mary Major, Diana McMillen, Mary Jo Plutt, Maureen Powers, Martha Schiel, Linda Foley Woodrum
Recipe Development Editor Marion Viall
Test Kitchen Director Sharon Stilwell
Test Kitchen Photo Studio Director Janet Pittman
Test Kitchen Home Economists Lynn Blanchard, Jean Brekke, Kay Cargill, Marilyn Cornelius, Jennifer Darling, Maryellyn Krantz, Lynelle Munn, Dianna Nolin, Marge Steenson
Associate Art Directors Linda Ford Vermie, Neoma Alt West, Randall Yontz
Assistant Art Directors Lynda Haupert, Harijs Priekulis, Tom Wegner
Senior Graphic Designers Jack Murphy, Stan Sams, Darla Whipple-Frain
Graphic Designers Mike Burns, Blake Welch, Brian Wignall

Vice President, Editorial Director Doris Eby
Executive Director, Editorial Services Duane L. Gregg

President, Book Group Fred Stines
Director of Publishing Robert B. Nelson
Vice President, Retail Marketing Jamie Martin
Vice President, Direct Marketing Arthur Heydendael

Cookies
Editor Maureen Powers
Copy and Production Editor Marsha Jahns
Graphic Designer Lynda Haupert
Electronic Text Processor Paula Forest
Photographers Michael Jensen and Sean Fitzgerald
Food Stylists Suzanne Finley, Carol Grones, Dianna Nolin, Janet Pittman

On the cover
Rosettes (see recipe, page 112), Whole Wheat-Peanut Butter
Blossoms (see recipe, page 44), Old-Fashioned Chocolate Chippers
(see recipe, page 30), and Pistachio Pinwheels (see recipe, page 90)

Our seal assures you that every recipe in *Cookies*
has been tested in the Better Homes and Gardens® Test Kitchen.
This means that each recipe is practical and reliable,
and meets our high standards of taste appeal.

Mmmm . . . there's nothing quite like the enticing aroma of warm cookies. Quiet your cookie cravings with homemade nut cookies, zesty spice cookies, or rich, dark chocolate cookies. Chewy and crisp, big and small, this collection of cookies has it all.

In *Cookies* you'll find the best of the best drop cookies, bar cookies, cookie cones, cutout cookies, and deep-fried cookies. And with the helpful hints on cookie making we've included, baking batches of your favorite sweet treats will be even easier.

So come on! Savor the flavors and the sweet tastes of success with these sensational recipes.

Contents

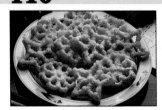

Delicate and delicious—gooey and good-tasting. These show-off bar cookies are impossible to resist.

Bake these stir-and-drop doughs into crispy, chewy, or cakey cookie jar classics.

Eyes will open wide at the sight of these bigger-than-life delights.

Bet you can't eat just one! You'll have to try all seven of these hand-shaped cookie creations.

What's easier than refrigerated rolls of dough, ready and waiting for you to bake on a moment's notice?

Surprise! A first-class filling is tucked inside each of these fabulous gems.

Roll up enticing fillings in cookie dough for a kaleidoscope of cookie flavors.

In the wink of an eye and the flick of a wrist, you've got buttery-rich spritz cookies.

Special Helps
Follow our culinary clues to solve the puzzle of successful cookie baking.

Special Helps
Wherever your cookie gifts are headed—keep our packing and wrapping guidelines in mind.

No-Bake Goodies

"Just what do you make of it, Watson? Are these no-bake beauties cookies or candy? Or both?"

You don't have to be Sherlock Holmes to solve this luscious puzzler. Their double identity lets them be whatever you want— cookie *or* candy.

So when you're tracking clues, searching for a super-simple, no-fuss, fix-'em-fast treat, start here.

Crisp Peanut Balls and Choco-Peanut Squares

Crisp Peanut Balls

½ cup sugar
½ cup light corn syrup
1 cup peanut butter
3 cups crisp rice cereal

Line a cookie sheet with waxed paper. Set aside. Combine sugar and corn syrup. Cook and stir till sugar is dissolved (see photo 1). Stir in peanut butter till melted. Remove from heat. Add cereal, stirring till combined (see photo 2). Drop by rounded teaspoons onto the prepared cookie sheet. *Or,* shape into 1-inch balls (see photo 3). Makes about 64.

Choco-Peanut Squares: Prepare Crisp Peanut Balls as above, *except* line a 9x9x2-inch baking pan with foil, extending foil over edges of pan. Press cereal mixture into prepared pan (see photo 4). Sprinkle one 6-ounce package (1 cup) miniature *semisweet chocolate pieces* over the top. Let stand for 5 minutes. Spread softened chocolate pieces over cereal mixture. Chill about 30 minutes. Lift cereal mixture out of pan. Peel off foil. Cut into squares. Makes 36.

1 As you cook the sugar and corn syrup mixture, stir it constantly, but gently, so it doesn't splash on the sides of the saucepan. When the sugar dissolves completely, no grains will be visible; the mixture will be a clear syrup, as shown.

2 Add the cereal to the pan a little bit at a time. That way, it all becomes well coated with the peanut butter mixture.

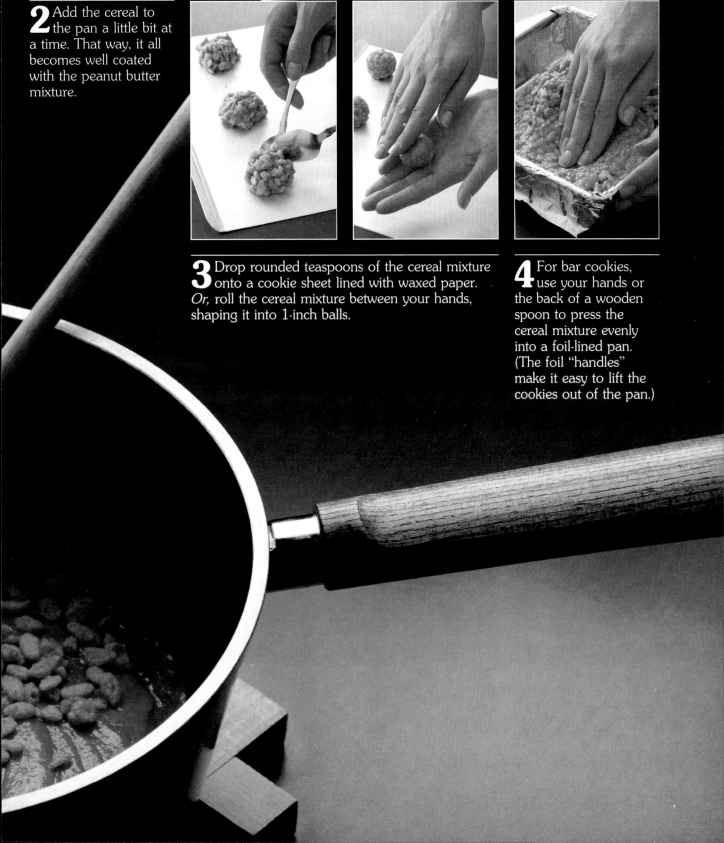

3 Drop rounded teaspoons of the cereal mixture onto a cookie sheet lined with waxed paper. *Or,* roll the cereal mixture between your hands, shaping it into 1-inch balls.

4 For bar cookies, use your hands or the back of a wooden spoon to press the cereal mixture evenly into a foil-lined pan. (The foil "handles" make it easy to lift the cookies out of the pan.)

Cinnamon-Marshmallow Squares

1 **10-ounce package marshmallows**
¼ **cup butter** *or* **margarine**
4 **cups crisp rice cereal**
2 **cups cornflakes, slightly crushed**
½ **cup red cinnamon candies** *or* **raisins**

Line a 9x9x2-inch baking pan with foil, extending foil over the edges of the pan. Butter the foil. Set pan aside.

In a large saucepan melt marshmallows and butter or margarine over low heat, stirring constantly. Remove pan from heat. Add rice cereal, cornflakes, and cinnamon candies or raisins, stirring till combined (see photo 2, page 9). Press mixture evenly into prepared pan (see photo 4, page 9). Let stand till firm. Use the foil to lift mixture out of pan. Peel off the foil. Cut into squares. Makes 18.

Tropical Fruit Balls

½ **of a 6-ounce can (⅓ cup) pineapple juice concentrate, thawed**
3 **tablespoons light corn syrup**
2½ **cups finely crushed vanilla wafers (about 65 wafers)**
1 **cup chopped raisins**
½ **cup chopped almonds** *or* **macadamia nuts, toasted**
Sifted powdered sugar *or* **finely crushed vanilla wafers**

In a large bowl stir together thawed concentrate and corn syrup. Add the 2½ cups crushed vanilla wafers, stirring till combined (see photo 2, page 9). Add raisins and almonds or macadamia nuts. Mix with hands till combined.

Shape the fruit mixture into 1-inch balls (see photo 3, page 9). Roll balls in powdered sugar or crushed wafers to coat. Store tightly covered in the refrigerator. Makes about 60.

Chocolate Rum Balls

Make these dried fruit confections ahead and store them in the freezer for up to a month. Just before serving, spruce them up a bit by rerolling them in sugar.

¼ **cup honey**
3 **tablespoons rum** *or* **orange juice**
1 **8½-ounce package chocolate wafers, finely crushed**
1 **6-ounce package dried apricots, finely snipped**
Sugar

In a large mixing bowl stir together honey and rum or orange juice. Add crushed wafers and apricots, stirring till combined (see photo 2, page 9). Shape into 1-inch balls (see photo 3, page 9). Roll balls in sugar. Makes about 40.

Rocky Road Drops

For a festive splash of color, use colored marshmallows in these candylike cookies.

1 **6-ounce package (1 cup) semisweet chocolate pieces**
6 **ounces chocolate-** *or* **vanilla-flavored confectioners' coating, cut up**
1½ **cups peanut butter cereal**
1 **cup tiny marshmallows**
¾ **cup peanuts**

Line a cookie sheet with waxed paper. Set aside. In a medium heavy saucepan melt chocolate pieces and confectioners' coating over low heat, stirring often. Remove pan from heat.

In a medium mixing bowl stir together cereal, marshmallows, and peanuts. Add cereal mixture to melted chocolate, stirring till combined (see photo 2, page 9). Drop by rounded teaspoons onto the prepared cookie sheet (see photo 3, page 9). Chill about 1 hour or till firm. Store tightly covered in the refrigerator. Makes about 36.

Bar Cookie Arithmetic

Bar cookies may be cut into a variety of shapes and sizes. The number of bars a recipe yields depends on the size of the pan as well as the size of the portion. As a general rule, the thicker the bar, the smaller it should be cut. Likewise, the richer the bar, the smaller the serving.

Use the table below as a guide for cutting bar cookies. The size of the bar or square is approximate and will vary with your pans.

Baking Pan Size	Number of Cuts		Approximate Size of Bar	Number of Bars
	Lengthwise	Crosswise		
8x8x2 inches	3	3	2x2 inches	16
	3	4	2x1½ inches	20
	4	4	1½x1½ inches	25
	3	7	2x1 inch	32
9x9x2 inches	2	5	3x1½ inches	18
	3	5	2¼x1½ inches	24
	5	5	1½x1½ inches	36
11x7x1½ inches	3	3	1¾x2¾ inches	16
	4	3	1⅜x2¾ inches	20
	4	4	1⅜x2¼ inches	25
	3	7	1¾x1⅜ inches	32
13x9x2 inches	3	7	2¼x1⅝ inches	32
	5	5	1½x2⅛ inches	36
	5	7	1½x1⅝ inches	48
15x10x1 inches	3	7	2½x1⅞ inches	32
	3	11	2½x1¼ inches	48
	7	8	1¼x1¾ inches	72

Batter Bars And Brownies

Quick, easy, and irresistible—now that's a cookie worth investing in. These priceless cookies are gems because they require no rolling, no cutting, no dropping, and no shaping.

Simply stir together the batter for these yummy bar cookies and brownies, and bake. You'll want to protect these jewels. But don't—it's fun sharing your wealth!

Citrus-Yogurt Squares

Citrus-Yogurt Squares

1¼ **cups all-purpose flour**
 1 **teaspoon baking powder**
 ¼ **teaspoon baking soda**
 6 **tablespoons butter *or* margarine**
 1 **cup sugar**
 1 **egg**
 1 **teaspoon finely shredded lemon peel**
    ***or* orange peel**
 4 **teaspoons lemon juice *or* orange juice**
 ½ **cup plain, lemon, *or* orange yogurt**
 1 **cup sifted powdered sugar**

Grease a 9x9x2-inch baking pan. Set aside. In a medium mixing bowl stir together flour, baking powder, and soda (see photo 1). Set aside.

In a medium saucepan melt butter or margarine. Remove from heat. Stir in sugar. Add egg, *½ teaspoon* lemon peel or orange peel, and *1 teaspoon* lemon juice or orange juice. Beat well. Stir in yogurt (see photo 2). Gradually add flour mixture, beating till combined. Spread batter into the prepared pan (see photo 3).

Bake in a 350° oven for 25 to 30 minutes or till a wooden toothpick inserted in center comes out clean (see photo 4). Cool completely on a wire rack.

For glaze, in a small mixing bowl stir together powdered sugar, remaining ½ teaspoon lemon peel or orange peel, and remaining 3 teaspoons lemon juice or orange juice. Spread glaze over top. Cut into squares (see photo 5). Makes 18.

1 Stir the dry ingredients together in a medium-size mixing bowl. Mix well to evenly distribute any leavenings (baking powder and/or baking soda) and spices.

2 Stir in the yogurt last, when there's no chance of it becoming too hot and breaking down. Vanilla is also added at the end so its flavor doesn't evaporate.

3 As you spread the batter into the prepared pan, make sure it's about the same distance from the top of the pan on all sides and that the center is level with the edges. The bars will look more attractive and bake more evenly.

4 To tell if cakelike bars are done, stick a wooden toothpick near the center of the bars. If the toothpick comes out clean, the bars are ready to come out of the oven.

5 So you don't end up with crooked bars and brownies, use a ruler to measure and mark the bars into the size pieces you want. Then stick in toothpicks so you know where to cut.

Some bars need to be cut while still warm to prevent cracking or shattering; others need to cool completely before cutting. Follow the directions given in each recipe.

Carrot Bars

Complete with Cream Cheese Frosting, these spicy bars are like tiny pieces of carrot cake.

1⅓   **cups all-purpose flour**
1½   **teaspoons baking powder**
1½   **teaspoons ground cinnamon**
 ¼   **teaspoon baking soda**
 ¼   **teaspoon ground nutmeg**
 ⅛   **teaspoon ground cloves**
 3   **eggs**
1½   **cups finely shredded carrot**
 1   **cup sugar·**
 ¾   **cup cooking oil**
 ½   **cup raisins**
 ½   **cup chopped walnuts**
     Cream Cheese Frosting

In a medium mixing bowl stir together flour, baking powder, cinnamon, soda, nutmeg, and cloves (see photo 1, page 14). Set aside.

In a large mixer bowl combine eggs, carrot, sugar, and oil. Beat with an electric mixer till combined. Gradually add flour mixture, beating till combined. Stir in raisins and walnuts.

Spread the batter evenly into an ungreased 15x10x1-inch baking pan (see photo 3, page 15). Bake in a 350° oven for 25 to 30 minutes or till a wooden toothpick inserted in center comes out clean (see photo 4, page 15). Cool completely on a wire rack.

Frost with Cream Cheese Frosting. Cut into bars (see photo 5, page 15). Store tightly covered in the refrigerator. Makes 48.

Cream Cheese Frosting: In a small mixer bowl beat one 3-ounce package *cream cheese,* softened; ¼ cup *butter or margarine;* and 1 teaspoon *vanilla* with an electric mixer on medium speed till light and fluffy. Gradually beat in 2 cups sifted *powdered sugar* till smooth.

Maple-Pecan Bars

 1   **cup all-purpose flour**
 ½   **teaspoon baking powder**
 ⅓   **cup butter *or* margarine**
 ½   **cup sugar**
 1   **egg**
 1   **teaspoon vanilla**
 ⅓   **cup maple-flavored syrup**
 ¼   **cup milk**
 ¾   **cup chopped pecans**
     Powdered sugar (optional)

Grease a 9x9x2-inch baking pan. Set aside. In a small mixing bowl stir together flour and baking powder (see photo 1, page 14). Set aside.

In a small mixer bowl beat butter or margarine with an electric mixer on medium speed for 30 seconds. Add sugar and beat till fluffy (see photo 1, page 31). Add egg and vanilla and beat well. Beat in syrup and milk (mixture will appear curdled). Gradually add flour mixture, beating till combined. Stir in pecans.

Spread batter into the prepared pan (see photo 3, page 15). Bake in a 350° oven for 25 to 30 minutes or till a wooden toothpick inserted in center comes out clean (see photo 4, page 15). Cool completely on a wire rack. Sift powdered sugar over cookies, if desired. Cut into bars (see photo 5, page 15). Makes 24.

Chocolate Syrup Brownies

A mere 15 minutes in the kitchen and you can have rich, fudgy brownies ready to pop into the oven. In another 45 minutes or so, you can enjoy one with a glass of cold milk.

1¼ **cups all-purpose flour**
¼ **teaspoon salt**
½ **cup butter *or* margarine**
1 **cup sugar**
4 **eggs**
1 **16-ounce can (about 1½ cups) chocolate-flavored syrup**
1 **cup chopped nuts**
  Quick Chocolate Glaze

In a small mixing bowl stir together flour and salt (see photo 1, page 14). Set aside.

In a large mixer bowl beat butter or margarine with an electric mixer for 30 seconds. Add sugar and beat till fluffy (see photo 1, page 31). Add eggs and beat well. Stir in chocolate-flavored syrup. Gradually stir in flour mixture (mixture will appear curdled). Stir in nuts.

Spread batter into an ungreased 13x9x2-inch baking pan (see photo 3, page 15). Bake in a 350° oven for 30 to 35 minutes or till a wooden toothpick inserted in center comes out clean (see photo 4, page 15). Cool slightly on a wire rack. Top with Quick Chocolate Glaze. Cool completely. Cut into bars (see photo 5, page 15). Makes 32.

Quick Chocolate Glaze: In a medium saucepan combine ⅔ cup *sugar,* 3 tablespoons *milk,* and 3 tablespoons *butter or margarine.* Cook and stir over medium heat till mixture is boiling. Boil for 30 seconds. Remove from heat. Stir in ½ cup *semisweet chocolate pieces* till melted.

Chewy Ginger Bars

2 **cups all-purpose flour**
2 **teaspoons baking powder**
1 **teaspoon ground ginger**
1 **teaspoon ground cinnamon**
¼ **teaspoon ground cloves**
½ **cup butter *or* margarine**
1¾ **cups packed brown sugar**
2 **eggs**
¼ **cup molasses**
1 **teaspoon vanilla**
  Powdered sugar

Grease a 13x9x2-inch baking pan. Set aside. In a large mixing bowl stir together flour, baking powder, ginger, cinnamon, and cloves (see photo 1, page 14). Set aside.

In a saucepan melt butter or margarine. Remove from heat. Stir in brown sugar. Add eggs, one at a time, stirring till combined. Stir in molasses and vanilla. Gradually add flour mixture, stirring till combined.

Spread batter into the prepared pan (see photo 3, page 15). Bake in a 350° oven for 20 to 25 minutes or till a wooden toothpick inserted in center comes out clean (see photo 4, page 15). Cool completely on a wire rack. Sift powdered sugar over cookies. Cut into bars (see photo 5, page 15). Makes 32.

Butterscotch Blonde Brownies

We added butterscotch pieces to these blonde brownies for a double-delicious dose of butterscotch flavor.

1½ cups all-purpose flour
½ cup quick-cooking rolled oats
2 teaspoons baking powder
½ cup butter *or* margarine
2 cups packed brown sugar
2 eggs
1 teaspoon vanilla
½ cup chopped pecans
½ cup butterscotch-flavored pieces
½ cup coconut

Grease a 13x9x2-inch baking pan. Set aside. In a medium mixing bowl stir together flour, rolled oats, and baking powder (see photo 1, page 14). Set aside.

In a large saucepan melt butter or margarine. Remove from heat. Stir in sugar. Add eggs, one at a time, stirring till combined. Stir in vanilla (see photo 2, page 14).

Gradually add flour mixture, beating till combined. Stir in pecans, butterscotch-flavored pieces, and coconut. Spread batter into the prepared pan (see photo 3, page 15).

Bake in a 350° oven for 20 to 25 minutes or till a wooden toothpick inserted in center comes out clean (see photo 4, page 15). Cut into bars while warm (see photo 5, page 15). Cool completely on a wire rack. Makes 32.

Cocoa Cake Brownies

1½ cups all-purpose flour
¾ cup unsweetened cocoa powder
1 teaspoon baking powder
¼ teaspoon baking soda
¾ cup butter *or* margarine
1¼ cups sugar
2 eggs
1 teaspoon vanilla
1 cup milk
1 cup chopped walnuts
Cocoa Frosting

Grease a 15x10x1-inch baking pan. Set aside. In a medium mixing bowl stir together flour, cocoa powder, baking powder, and soda (see photo 1, page 14). Set aside.

In a large mixer bowl beat butter or margarine with an electric mixer on medium speed for 30 seconds. Add sugar and beat till fluffy (see photo 1, page 31). Add eggs and vanilla and beat well. Add flour mixture and milk alternately to the beaten mixture, beating after each addition. Stir in walnuts.

Spread batter into the prepared pan (see photo 3, page 15). Bake in a 350° oven about 18 minutes or till a wooden toothpick inserted in center comes out clean (see photo 4, page 15). Cool completely on a wire rack. Frost with Cocoa Frosting. Cut into bars (see photo 5, page 15). Makes 32.

Cocoa Frosting: In a medium heavy saucepan combine ⅓ cup *butter or margarine* and 3 tablespoons *milk*. Cook and stir over low heat till butter or margarine melts. Stir in 3 cups sifted *powdered sugar* and ⅓ cup *unsweetened cocoa powder,* sifted. Add additional *milk,* if necessary, to make frosting spreadable.

▶ *Pictured opposite: Butterscotch Blonde Brownies and Cocoa Cake Brownies*

Bars with A Crust

As the cookie foreman of your baking crew, it's your job to oversee the construction of these cookies—beginning with their tasty foundation.

A rich cookie crust supports the tempting topping on these oh-so-scrumptious bars.

When the cookies are finished baking, call in the wrecking crew to help demolish a whole plate of them.

Apricot Bars

Apricot Bars

½ of a 6-ounce package (¾ cup) dried
   apricots, snipped
½ cup water
¼ cup packed brown sugar
1 tablespoon all-purpose flour
½ teaspoon ground coriander
½ teaspoon vanilla
¾ cup all-purpose flour
½ cup packed brown sugar
½ cup quick-cooking rolled oats
⅓ cup whole bran cereal
⅓ cup butter *or* margarine
3 tablespoons water

In a small saucepan combine the dried apricots and the ½ cup water. Bring to boiling. Reduce the heat and simmer, covered, for 8 to 10 minutes or till tender.

Meanwhile, in a small mixing bowl combine the ¼ cup brown sugar, the 1 tablespoon flour, and coriander. Stir into apricot mixture. Cook and stir till thickened (see photo 1). Remove from heat and stir in vanilla (see photo 2, page 14).

For crust, in a medium mixing bowl stir together the ¾ cup flour, the ½ cup brown sugar, oats, and bran cereal. Cut in butter or margarine till crumbly (see photo 2). Reserve *½ cup* of the crust mixture for topping. Stir the 3 tablespoons water into the remaining crust mixture.

Press crust mixture evenly into the bottom of an ungreased 8x8x2-inch baking dish (see photo 3). Spread apricot mixture evenly over crust (see photo 4). Sprinkle reserved crust mixture over the top, pressing in lightly. Bake in a 350° oven for 30 to 35 minutes or till golden. Cool completely on a wire rack. Cut into bars (see photo 5, page 15). Makes 25.

1 Cook the apricot mixture over low heat till it becomes very thick. Stir constantly, using a figure-8 motion, to prevent sticking and scorching, and to help the mixture cook evenly.

2 With a pastry blender, use an up-and-down motion to mix the butter or margarine into the flour-oat mixture. Stop once in a while and scrape off any butter that sticks to the pastry blender.

3 For bars with a crumb or dough crust, press the mixture into the pan with your hands. Make sure it's the same thickness in all areas for even baking.

4 Pour the apricot mixture over the crust. Using a spoon, spread it evenly to the edges.

Luscious Lemon Diamonds

⅓ cup butter *or* margarine
¼ cup sugar
½ teaspoon finely shredded lemon peel
1 cup all-purpose flour
6 eggs
1½ cups sugar
1 teaspoon finely shredded lemon peel
½ cup lemon juice
2 tablespoons all-purpose flour
1 teaspoon baking powder
Powdered sugar

Grease an 11x7x1½-inch baking pan. Set aside. For crust, beat butter with an electric mixer for 30 seconds. Add the ¼ cup sugar and the ½ teaspoon lemon peel; beat till fluffy (see photo 1, page 31). Gradually add the 1 cup flour; beat till crumbly. Press crust mixture evenly into the bottom of the prepared pan (see photo 3, page 23). Bake in a 350° oven for 20 minutes.

Beat eggs, sugar, the 1 teaspoon lemon peel, lemon juice, the 2 tablespoons flour, and baking powder till combined. Continue beating about 3 minutes or till slightly thickened (mixture may be foamy). Spread evenly over hot crust (see photo 4, page 23). Return to oven; bake about 25 minutes more or till set. Cool. Just before serving, sift powdered sugar over cookies. Cut into diamonds (see tip, below). Makes about 25.

Chocolate-Pecan Bars

A yummy chocolate variation of the ever-popular Southern-style pecan pie.

½ cup butter *or* margarine
2 tablespoons sugar
1½ cups all-purpose flour
2 eggs
½ cup packed brown sugar
½ cup chopped pecans
½ cup semisweet chocolate pieces
½ cup light corn syrup
2 tablespoons butter *or* margarine, melted
1 teaspoon vanilla

For crust, in a mixer bowl beat the ½ cup butter or margarine with an electric mixer on medium speed for 30 seconds. Add sugar and beat till fluffy (see photo 1, page 31). Stir in flour. Press crust mixture evenly into the bottom of an ungreased 11x7x1½-inch baking pan (see photo 3, page 23). Bake in a 350° oven 15 minutes.

Meanwhile, in a medium mixing bowl beat eggs slightly. Stir in brown sugar, pecans, chocolate pieces, corn syrup, the 2 tablespoons melted butter or margarine, and vanilla. Spread mixture evenly over hot crust (see photo 4, page 23). Return to oven and bake about 25 minutes more or till set. Cool completely on a wire rack. Cut into bars (see photo 5, page 15). Makes 25.

Cutting Cookies Down to Size

Make your cookie platter a little more interesting by cutting your bar cookies into diamond or triangle shapes.
● To make triangles, simply cut bars into squares, then halve them diagonally.
● For diamonds, first make straight parallel cuts 1 to 1½ inches apart down the length of your pan. Then make diagonal cuts across the pan (at a 45-degree angle), keeping the lines as even as you can. (You will have irregularly shaped pieces at each end of the pan that you can use to fill in small gaps on your cookie platter.)

Orange-Raisin Bars

No food processor? Run the fruit and nut mixture through the coarse plate of a food grinder instead.

1 medium orange
1 cup raisins
½ cup walnuts
¾ cup butter *or* margarine
¾ cup packed brown sugar
2½ cups all-purpose flour
1 tablespoon baking powder
2 eggs
¾ cup milk
Orange Butter Frosting
48 walnut halves

Grease a 13x9x2-inch baking pan. Set aside. Finely shred ¼ *teaspoon* orange peel and reserve for frosting. Halve the orange. Juice one half, reserving ¼ cup juice (add water, if necessary). Discard orange half. Cut up the remaining *unpeeled* orange half. Place cut-up orange, raisins, and the ½ cup walnuts in a food processor bowl. Cover and process till ground. Set aside.

For crust, beat butter or margarine with an electric mixer for 30 seconds. Add brown sugar and beat till fluffy (see photo 1, page 31). Gradually add flour, beating till crumbly. Press *2 cups* of the crust mixture evenly into bottom of the prepared pan (see photo 3, page 23). Stir baking powder into remaining crust mixture. Add reserved orange juice, eggs, and milk, beating till combined. Stir in ground orange mixture. Spread mixture evenly over crust (see photo 4, page 23). Bake in a 375° oven for 20 to 25 minutes or till brown. Cool completely on a wire rack. Frost with Orange Butter Frosting. Cut into bars (see photo 5, page 15). Garnish each bar with a walnut half. Makes 48.

Orange Butter Frosting: Beat ¼ cup *butter or margarine* till light and fluffy. Gradually add 1¼ cups sifted *powdered sugar,* beating well. Beat in 2 tablespoons *milk,* 1 teaspoon *vanilla,* and reserved orange peel. Gradually beat in 1¼ cups sifted *powdered sugar.* (Beat in additional *milk,* if necessary, to make spreadable.)

Peanut-Oat Bars

1 cup quick-cooking rolled oats
½ cup all-purpose flour
½ cup packed brown sugar
¼ teaspoon baking soda
⅓ cup butter *or* margarine, melted
1 3-ounce package cream cheese, softened
¼ cup peanut butter
¼ cup sugar
¼ cup milk
1 egg
½ cup chopped peanuts
⅓ cup semisweet chocolate pieces
2 teaspoons shortening

For crust, in a medium mixing bowl stir together oats, flour, brown sugar, and baking soda (see photo 1, page 14). Stir in the melted butter or margarine. Press the crust mixture evenly into bottom of an ungreased 11x7x1½-inch baking pan (see photo 3, page 23). Bake in a 350° oven for 8 minutes.

Meanwhile, in a small mixer bowl beat cream cheese and peanut butter with an electric mixer till smooth. Add sugar, milk, and egg and beat well. Stir in peanuts. Spread mixture evenly over hot crust (see photo 4, page 23). Return to oven and bake about 18 minutes more or till set. Cool on a wire rack for 5 minutes.

In a small heavy saucepan melt chocolate pieces and shortening over low heat till smooth. Drizzle over entire surface. Chill thoroughly. Cut into bars (see photo 5, page 15). Store tightly covered in the refrigerator. Makes 25.

Coffee 'n' Cream Bars

¼ **cup butter *or* margarine**
¼ **cup sugar**
2 **tablespoons coffee liqueur**
1 **cup all-purpose flour**
2 **teaspoons instant coffee crystals**
⅓ **cup whipping cream**
3 **eggs**
1 **cup sugar**
1 **tablespoon all-purpose flour**
1 **teaspoon vanilla**
½ **teaspoon baking powder**
½ **cup finely chopped walnuts *or* pecans**

For crust, in a small mixer bowl beat butter or margarine with an electric mixer on medium speed for 30 seconds. Add the ¼ cup sugar and beat till fluffy (see photo 1, page 31). Add coffee liqueur and beat well. Stir in the 1 cup flour. Press mixture evenly into the bottom of an ungreased 11x7x1½-inch baking pan (see photo 3, page 23). Bake in a 350° oven 12 minutes.

Meanwhile, in a large mixer bowl dissolve coffee crystals in whipping cream. Add eggs, the 1 cup sugar, the 1 tablespoon flour, vanilla, and baking powder and beat well. Spread mixture evenly over hot crust (see photo 4, page 23). Sprinkle with chopped nuts.

Return to oven and bake for 20 to 25 minutes more or till set in center. Cool completely on a wire rack. Cut into bars (see photo 5, page 15). Store tightly covered in refrigerator. Makes 25.

Mocha Cheesecake Bars

The cookie-crumb crust softens slightly if you store these bars overnight.

1½ **cups finely crushed chocolate wafers (about 30 wafers)**
¼ **cup butter *or* margarine, melted**
1 **8-ounce package cream cheese, softened**
⅔ **cup sugar**
¼ **cup milk**
3 **tablespoons unsweetened cocoa powder**
3 **eggs**
3 **tablespoons strong coffee**

Grease an 11x7x1½-inch baking pan. Set aside. For crust, in a medium mixing bowl stir together crushed wafers and melted butter or margarine. Press crust mixture evenly into the bottom of the prepared pan (see photo 3, page 23).

In a small mixer bowl beat cream cheese till fluffy. Add sugar, milk, and cocoa powder and beat till combined. Add eggs and coffee, beating just till combined. *Do not overbeat.*

Spread cream cheese mixture evenly over crust (see photo 4, page 23). Bake in a 350° oven for 30 to 35 minutes or till center appears set. Cool on a wire rack. Chill thoroughly. Cut into bars (see photo 5, page 15). Makes 25.

▶ *Pictured opposite: Mocha Cheesecake Bars*

Delightful Drops

Step right up for one of the greatest treats on earth! As ringmaster of this cookie extravaganza, you'll please any crowd with these three-ring favorites.

In the center ring, lover's of chewy cookies will ooh and ah at Old-Fashioned Chocolate Chippers. Sour Cream Apricot Drops tame those who prefer tender, cakelike cookies. And, for anyone who likes a crisp drop cookie, take a chance on Oatmeal Wheat Treats.

No clowning around, all three of these drop cookies promise a performance worthy of an encore.

*Old-Fashioned
Chocolate Chippers*

Old-Fashioned Chocolate Chippers

2½	cups all-purpose flour
1	teaspoon baking soda
½	cup butter *or* margarine
½	cup shortening
1	cup packed brown sugar
½	cup sugar
2	eggs
1½	teaspoons vanilla
1	12-ounce package (2 cups) semisweet chocolate pieces
1	cup chopped walnuts *or* pecans

In a medium mixing bowl stir together flour and baking soda (see photo 1, page 14). Set aside.

In a large mixer bowl beat butter or margarine and shortening with an electric mixer on medium speed for 30 seconds. Add brown sugar and sugar and beat till fluffy (see photo 1). Add eggs and vanilla and beat well. Gradually add flour mixture, beating till combined. Stir in chocolate pieces and nuts.

Drop by rounded teaspoons 2 inches apart onto an ungreased cookie sheet (see photo 2). Bake in a 375° oven for 8 to 10 minutes or till bottoms are lightly browned (see photo 3). Cool on cookie sheet for 1 minute. Remove; cool completely on wire racks (see photo 4). Makes 60.

Oatmeal Chippers: Prepare Old-Fashioned Chocolate Chippers as above, *except* use *1½ cups* all-purpose flour and add 2 cups *quick-cooking rolled oats.*

Double-Wheat Chippers: Prepare Old-Fashioned Chocolate Chippers as above, *except* use *1 cup* all-purpose flour and add 1 cup *whole wheat flour* and 1 cup *unprocessed wheat bran.*

1 Beat the butter or margarine and shortening together till creamy. Add the sugars and continue beating till the mixture is light and fluffy, as shown. Use a rubber scraper to scrape the sides of the bowl.

2 Scoop up the cookie dough in a spoon. Use the back of another spoon to push the dough off the spoon. (*Or,* use a cookie dough dropper, a tool like the one pictured. It's available at kitchen gadget shops.) The dough will spread while it's baking, so drop the mounds about 2 inches apart.

3 Drop cookies are done when the dough is set and the bottoms are lightly browned. For chocolate cookies, however, test for doneness by lightly touching the top of a cookie with your fingertip. If they're done, the imprint will be barely visible. If they're not done, the imprint will be large and the cookies will be doughy.

4 Use a pancake turner or wide metal spatula to transfer the cookies from the cookie sheet to wire racks. Don't store or frost the cookies till they're completely cooled.

Double-Chocolate Chunk Specials

Dark-chocolate lovers can substitute five 1½-ounce bars of dark sweet chocolate for the milk chocolate or the semisweet chocolate pieces.

2½ **cups all-purpose flour**
⅓ **cup unsweetened cocoa powder**
1 **teaspoon baking soda**
½ **cup butter *or* margarine**
½ **cup shortening**
1 **cup packed brown sugar**
½ **cup sugar**
2 **eggs**
1½ **teaspoons vanilla**
1 **8-ounce bar milk chocolate, coarsely chopped, *or* one 12-ounce package (2 cups) semisweet chocolate pieces**

In a medium mixing bowl stir together flour, cocoa powder, and baking soda (see photo 1, page 14). Set aside.

In a large mixer bowl beat butter or margarine and shortening with an electric mixer on medium speed for 30 seconds. Add brown sugar and sugar and beat till fluffy (see photo 1, page 31). Add eggs and vanilla and beat well. Gradually add flour mixture, beating till combined. Stir in milk chocolate or semisweet chocolate.

Drop by rounded teaspoons 2 inches apart onto an ungreased cookie sheet (see photo 2, page 31). Bake in a 375° oven about 8 minutes or till a slight finger imprint remains (see photo 3, page 31). Cool on cookie sheet for 1 minute. Remove and cool completely on wire racks (see photo 4, page 31). Makes about 60.

Apple Pie Cookies

All the mouth-watering flavors of Mom's homemade apple pie—right here in these tender, totable cookies.

2 **cups all-purpose flour**
1 **teaspoon baking powder**
1 **teaspoon ground cinnamon**
¼ **teaspoon baking soda**
¼ **teaspoon ground nutmeg**
⅛ **teaspoon ground cloves**
½ **cup butter *or* margarine**
1 **cup sugar**
2 **eggs**
1 **large apple, peeled, cored, and shredded (1 cup)**
4 **teaspoons sugar**
¼ **teaspoon ground cinnamon**

Lightly grease a cookie sheet. Set aside. In a mixing bowl stir together flour, baking powder, the 1 teaspoon cinnamon, soda, nutmeg, and cloves (see photo 1, page 14). Set aside.

In a large mixer bowl beat butter or margarine with an electric mixer on medium speed for 30 seconds. Add the 1 cup sugar and beat till fluffy (see photo 1, page 31). Add eggs and beat well. Stir in shredded apple. Gradually add flour mixture, beating till combined.

Drop by rounded teaspoons 2 inches apart onto the prepared cookie sheet (see photo 2, page 31). Stir together the 4 teaspoons sugar and the ¼ teaspoon cinnamon. Sprinkle cinnamon-sugar mixture over tops of cookie dough.

Bake in a 375° oven for 8 to 10 minutes or till bottoms are lightly browned (see photo 3, page 31). Cool on cookie sheet for 1 minute. Remove and cool completely on wire racks (see photo 4, page 31). Makes about 40.

Oatmeal Wheat Treats

For more natural sweetness, add ½ cup raisins when stirring in the nuts.

- ½ cup all-purpose flour
- ½ cup whole wheat flour
- ¼ teaspoon baking soda
- ¼ cup butter *or* margarine
- ¼ cup shortening
- ⅓ cup sugar
- ⅓ cup packed brown sugar
- 1 egg
- 2 tablespoons milk
- ½ teaspoon vanilla
- 1 cup quick-cooking rolled oats
- ¼ cup chopped walnuts

Lightly grease a cookie sheet. Set aside. In a small mixing bowl stir together all-purpose flour, whole wheat flour, and baking soda (see photo 1, page 14). Set aside.

In a large mixer bowl beat butter or margarine and shortening with an electric mixer on medium speed for 30 seconds. Add sugar and brown sugar and beat till fluffy (see photo 1, page 31). Add egg, milk, and vanilla and beat well. Gradually add flour mixture, beating till combined. Stir in oats and nuts.

Drop by rounded teaspoons 2 inches apart onto the prepared cookie sheet (see photo 2, page 31). Bake in a 375° oven about 10 minutes or till bottoms are lightly browned (see photo 3, page 31). Cool on cookie sheet for 1 minute. Remove and cool completely on wire racks (see photo 4, page 31). Makes about 36.

Hazelnut-Mocha Marvels

- ¼ cup all-purpose flour
- 1 teaspoon ground cinnamon
- ¼ teaspoon baking powder
- 1 12-ounce package (2 cups) semisweet chocolate pieces
- 2 squares (2 ounces) unsweetened chocolate
- 2 tablespoons instant coffee crystals
- 2 tablespoons butter *or* margarine
- 2 eggs
- ⅔ cup packed brown sugar
- 1 teaspoon vanilla
- 1 cup chopped hazelnuts (filberts) *or* walnuts

Lightly grease a cookie sheet. Set aside. In a mixing bowl combine flour, cinnamon, and baking powder (see photo 1, page 14). Set aside.

In a medium heavy saucepan heat *1 cup* of the chocolate pieces, unsweetened chocolate, coffee crystals, and butter or margarine over low heat till melted, stirring constantly. Transfer to a small mixer bowl and cool slightly.

Add eggs, brown sugar, and vanilla to chocolate mixture and beat well. Gradually add flour mixture, beating till combined. Stir in remaining chocolate pieces and nuts.

Drop by heaping teaspoons 2 inches apart onto the prepared cookie sheet (see photo 2, page 31). Bake in a 350° oven for 8 to 10 minutes or till a slight finger imprint remains (see photo 3, page 31). Cool on cookie sheet for 1 minute. Remove and cool completely on wire racks (see photo 4, page 31). Makes about 30.

Coconut-Almond Marvels: Prepare Hazelnut-Mocha Marvels as above, *except* omit cinnamon, coffee crystals, and nuts. Stir ½ cup *coconut* and ½ cup slivered *almonds*, toasted, into the dough.

Sour Cream Apricot Drops

Because there's sour cream in both the dough and the frosting, store these cakelike cookies in the refrigerator.

1 cup all-purpose flour
¾ cup whole wheat flour
1 teaspoon baking powder
¼ teaspoon baking soda
¼ teaspoon ground allspice
⅛ teaspoon ground ginger
½ cup butter *or* margarine
½ cup sugar
½ cup packed brown sugar
1 egg
½ teaspoon vanilla
½ cup dairy sour cream
1 6-ounce package dried apricots, snipped
   Sour Cream Frosting

Lightly grease a cookie sheet. Set aside. In a medium mixing bowl stir together flours, baking powder, baking soda, allspice, and ginger (see photo 1, page 14). Set aside.

In a large mixer bowl beat butter or margarine with an electric mixer on medium speed for 30 seconds. Add sugar and brown sugar; beat till fluffy (see photo 1, page 31). Add egg and vanilla and beat well. Gradually add flour mixture and sour cream alternately to beaten mixture, beating well after each addition. Stir in apricots.

Drop by rounded teaspoons 2 inches apart onto the prepared cookie sheet (see photo 2, page 31). Bake in a 350° oven for 10 to 12 minutes or till bottoms are lightly browned (see photo 3, page 31). Cool on cookie sheet for 1 minute. Remove and cool completely on wire racks (see photo 4, page 31). Frost cookies with Sour Cream Frosting. Makes about 42.

Sour Cream Frosting: In a medium mixing bowl combine ¼ cup *dairy sour cream;* 2 tablespoons *butter or margarine,* softened; and ½ teaspoon *vanilla.* Gradually beat in 2 cups sifted *powdered sugar.* If necessary, add additional *powdered sugar* to make spreadable.

Rough and Ready Ranger Cookies

1¼ cups all-purpose flour
½ teaspoon baking soda
¼ teaspoon ground allspice
½ cup butter *or* margarine
⅔ cup packed brown sugar
⅓ cup sugar
1 egg
1 teaspoon vanilla
1 cup wheat flakes
½ cup coconut
½ cup chopped peanuts

In a mixing bowl stir together flour, baking soda, and allspice (see photo 1, page 14). Set aside.

In a large mixer bowl beat butter or margarine with an electric mixer on medium speed for 30 seconds. Add brown sugar and sugar and beat till fluffy (see photo 1, page 31). Add egg and vanilla and beat well. Gradually add flour mixture, beating till combined. Stir in wheat flakes, coconut, and peanuts.

Drop by rounded teaspoons 2 inches apart onto an ungreased cookie sheet (see photo 2, page 31). Bake in a 375° oven for 8 to 10 minutes or till bottoms are lightly browned (see photo 3, page 31). Cool on cookie sheet for 1 minute. Remove and cool completely on wire racks (see photo 4, page 31). Makes about 48.

◀ *Pictured opposite: Sour Cream Apricot Drops*

Monster Mouthfuls

Fee, fi, fo, fum, we smell a delicious cookie and we want one!

The next time you hear clamors for a super-duper treat, bake a fruity Ambrosia Cookie Pizza or a chewy Big Chipper Cookiewich.

Giant in both size and flavor, these monstrous cookies are a mouthful. Yet, even the most timid cook won't be scared off by these colossal cookies, because they're a snap to make.

Ambrosia Cookie Pizza

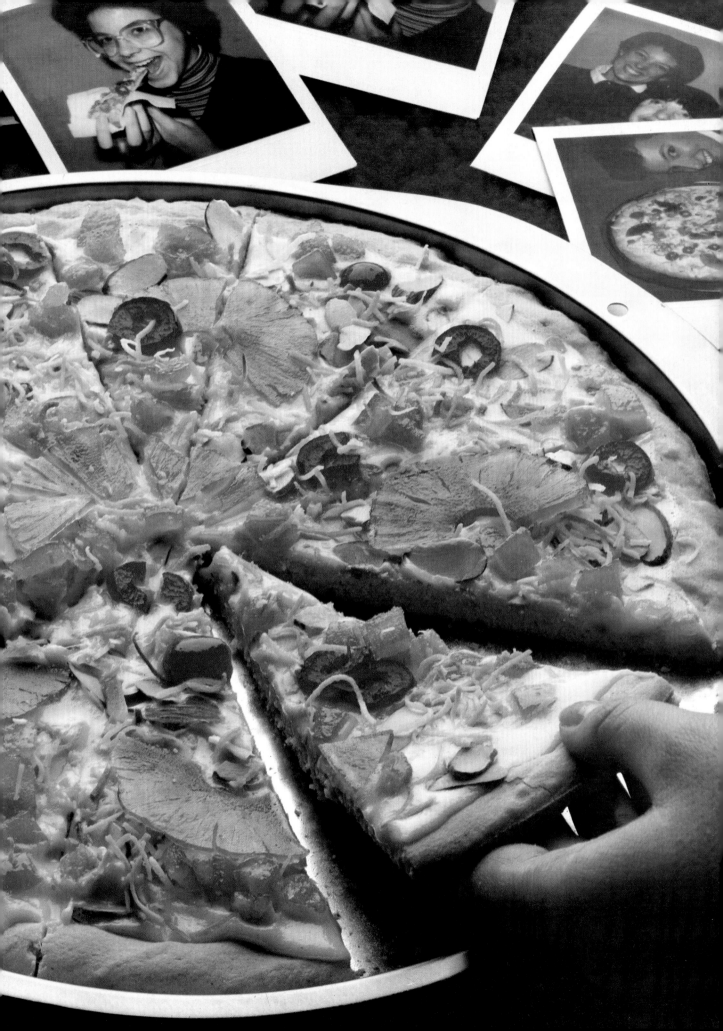

Ambrosia Cookie Pizza

Pizza party takes on a whole new meaning with this colorful dessert treat!

½ **cup butter *or* margarine**
⅓ **cup sugar**
⅓ **cup packed brown sugar**
1 **egg**
½ **teaspoon finely shredded orange peel**
2 **tablespoons orange juice**
1½ **cups all-purpose flour**
1 **3-ounce package cream cheese, softened**
1 **egg**
¼ **cup orange marmalade**
⅓ **cup sliced almonds, toasted**
⅓ **cup coconut, toasted**
⅓ **cup diced candied orange peel**
 Candied cherries, sliced (optional)
 Candied pineapple, halved (optional)

Lightly grease a 12-inch pizza pan. Set aside. For crust, in a large mixer bowl beat butter or margarine with an electric mixer on medium speed for 30 seconds. Add sugar and brown sugar and beat till fluffy (see photo 1, page 31). Add 1 egg, orange peel, and orange juice; beat well. Gradually add flour, beating till combined.

Spread crust mixture evenly into prepared pan (see photo 1). Bake in a 375° oven about 18 minutes or till golden brown.

Meanwhile, in a small mixer bowl beat together cream cheese, 1 egg, and orange marmalade (mixture will be thin). Spread cream cheese mixture evenly over hot crust to within ½ inch of edges (see photo 2). Sprinkle almonds, coconut, and candied orange peel over the top (see photo 3). Garnish with candied cherries and candied pineapple, if desired. Return cookie pizza to the oven and bake for 5 minutes more.

Cool completely in pan on a wire rack. Cut into wedges (see photo 4). Makes 16 servings.

1 Use a rubber scraper or a knife to spread the batter into a greased 12-inch pizza pan. As with bar cookies, spread the batter evenly so you'll have an evenly baked crust.

2 Spread the cream cheese mixture over the baked crust to within ½ inch of the edges. The mixture will be thin, so spread it carefully.

3 Scatter toasted almonds and coconut and candied orange peel over the cream cheese mixture. For more color, add candied cherries and candied pineapple slices, too.

4 Leave the cookie pizza in the pan and cool it completely on a wire rack. To serve, cut it into wedges with a sharp knife.

Big Chipper Cookiewich

1¼ **cups all-purpose flour**
  1 **teaspoon baking powder**
  ¼ **teaspoon baking soda**
  ¼ **cup butter *or* margarine**
  ¼ **cup shortening**
  ½ **cup packed brown sugar**
  ¼ **cup sugar**
  1 **egg**
  1 **teaspoon vanilla**
  1 **6-ounce package (1 cup) miniature semisweet chocolate pieces**
  1 **4-ounce container frozen whipped dessert topping, thawed**

Lightly grease two 9x1½-inch round baking pans. Set aside. In a medium mixing bowl stir together flour, baking powder, and baking soda (see photo 1, page 14). Set aside.

In a large mixer bowl beat butter or margarine and shortening with an electric mixer on medium speed for 30 seconds. Add brown sugar and sugar and beat till fluffy (see photo 1, page 31). Add egg and vanilla and beat well. Gradually add flour mixture, beating till combined. Stir in chocolate pieces.

Divide cookie dough in half. Spread each half into one of the prepared baking pans (see photo 1). Bake in a 350° oven for 15 to 17 minutes or till golden. Cool in baking pans for 5 minutes. Remove and cool completely on wire racks.

To assemble, place 1 cookie on a flat plate, bottom side up. Spread thawed dessert topping over the cookie. Carefully top with the second cookie, bottom side down. Cover tightly with foil. Chill several hours or overnight. Cut into wedges (see photo 4). Makes 16 servings.

Specially Hand Shaped

Hocus, pocus, mix it up—from plain dough to special cookie cut-ups. A little magic transforms every cookie dough into a one-of-a-kind creation.

Each cookie is shaped by hand, so it's extra-special. A little time and care is all it takes to make these magical munchies.

Watch out though! These hand-crafted cookies might disappear before your very eyes.

Peanut Butter Critters

Peanut Butter Critters

1¾ cups all-purpose flour
½ cup whole wheat flour
1½ teaspoons baking soda
1 cup peanut butter
½ cup butter *or* margarine
½ cup shortening
1½ cups sugar
½ cup packed brown sugar
2 eggs
1 teaspoon vanilla
Miniature semisweet chocolate pieces
Decorating Icing (optional)

In a medium mixing bowl combine flours and baking soda (see photo 1, page 14). Set aside.

In a large mixer bowl beat peanut butter, butter or margarine, and shortening with an electric mixer for 30 seconds. Add sugar and brown sugar and beat till fluffy (see photo 1, page 31). Add eggs and vanilla; beat well. Gradually stir or beat in flour mixture till combined (see photo 1).

Shape dough into balls and ropes (see photo 2). Arrange on an ungreased cookie sheet to form desired shapes. Flatten dough slightly and press together. Lightly press chocolate pieces into each cookie, creating eyes, buttons, or noses.

Bake in a 350° oven for 10 to 12 minutes or till edges are firm and bottoms are lightly browned (see photo 3). Cool on cookie sheet for 1 minute. Remove and cool completely on wire racks (see photo 4, page 31). If desired, pipe on bow ties or aprons with Decorating Icing. Makes about 36 large cookies.

Decorating Icing: Combine ½ cup sifted *powdered sugar* and enough *milk* (about 2 teaspoons) to make of piping consistency.

1 Work the dry ingredients into the beaten mixture in one of two ways. Simply stir the dry ingredients in with a wooden spoon or beat them in with an electric mixer.

If you're using a portable hand mixer, stir in the last half of the dry ingredients by hand. Otherwise, you risk burning out the mixer motor.

43

2 Shape the cookie dough into ropes by rolling it on the counter. *Or,* roll the dough between your palms into different sizes of balls.

3 Bake the cookies till the edges are firm and the bottoms are a light, golden brown (as shown). If the edges are doughy, bake the cookies a bit longer.

Honey 'n' Spice Cookies

You'll discover that these soft, cakelike cookies are close kin to ever-popular Snickerdoodles!

1¾ **cups all-purpose flour**
¼   **teaspoon baking soda**
¼   **teaspoon cream of tartar**
¼   **teaspoon ground nutmeg**
¼   **cup butter *or* margarine**
¼   **cup shortening**
⅔   **cup sugar**
1   **egg**
2   **tablespoons honey**
1   **teaspoon vanilla**
2   **tablespoons sugar**
½   **teaspoon ground cinnamon**

In a small mixing bowl stir together flour, baking soda, cream of tartar, and nutmeg (*see* photo 1, page 14). Set aside.

In a large mixer bowl beat butter or margarine and shortening with an electric mixer on medium speed for 30 seconds. Add the ⅔ cup sugar and beat till fluffy (*see* photo 1, page 31). Add egg, honey, and vanilla and beat well. Gradually stir or beat in flour mixture till combined (*see* photo 1, page 42).

Shape dough into 1¼-inch balls (*see* photo 2, page 43). In a pie plate or shallow bowl stir together the 2 tablespoons sugar and cinnamon. Roll balls in sugar-cinnamon mixture to coat. Place balls 2 inches apart on an ungreased cookie sheet. Flatten slightly with the bottom of a glass.

Bake in a 375° oven about 8 minutes or till edges are firm and bottoms are lightly browned (*see* photo 3, page 43). Remove and cool completely on wire racks (*see* photo 4, page 31). Makes about 36.

Whole Wheat-Peanut Butter Blossoms

1   **cup all-purpose flour**
¾   **cup whole wheat flour**
1   **teaspoon baking powder**
⅛   **teaspoon baking soda**
½   **cup shortening**
½   **cup peanut butter**
½   **cup sugar**
½   **cup packed brown sugar**
1   **egg**
2   **tablespoons milk**
1   **teaspoon vanilla**
½   **cup chopped peanuts**
    Sugar
    Milk chocolate kisses

In a medium mixing bowl stir together flours, baking powder, and baking soda (*see* photo 1, page 14). Set aside.

In a large mixer bowl beat shortening and peanut butter with an electric mixer on medium speed for 30 seconds. Add the ½ cup sugar and brown sugar and beat till fluffy (*see* photo 1, page 31). Add egg, milk, and vanilla; beat well. Gradually stir or beat in flour mixture till combined (*see* photo 1, page 42). Stir in peanuts.

Shape dough into 1-inch balls (*see* photo 2, page 43). Place additional sugar in a pie plate or shallow bowl. Roll balls in sugar to coat. Place balls 2 inches apart on an ungreased cookie sheet.

Bake in a 350° oven for 10 to 12 minutes or till edges are firm and bottoms are lightly browned (*see* photo 3, page 43). Immediately press a chocolate kiss into each cookie. Remove and cool completely on wire racks (*see* photo 4, page 31). Makes about 54.

▶   *Pictured opposite: Whole Wheat-Peanut Butter Blossoms*

David —
Love + Kisses
Lynda

Praline Sandies

We loaded our variation of this rich, buttery holiday classic with lots and lots of chopped pecans.

1 cup butter *or* margarine
⅓ cup packed brown sugar
1 tablespoon rum
1 teaspoon vanilla
2¼ cups all-purpose flour
1 cup chopped pecans
¼ cup sifted powdered sugar

In a large mixer bowl beat butter or margarine with an electric mixer on medium speed for 30 seconds. Add brown sugar and beat till fluffy (see photo 1, page 31). Add rum and vanilla and beat well. Gradually stir or beat in flour and pecans till combined (see photo 1, page 42).

Shape dough into 1-inch balls or 1½x½-inch ropes (see photo 2, page 43). Place 2 inches apart on an ungreased cookie sheet.

Bake in a 325° oven about 20 minutes or till edges are firm and bottoms are lightly browned (see photo 3, page 43). Remove and cool completely on wire racks (see photo 4, page 31). In a plastic bag gently shake a few at a time in powdered sugar. Makes about 48.

Old-Fashioned Sandies: Prepare Praline Sandies as above, *except* substitute *sugar* for the brown sugar, omit rum, and use 2 teaspoons *water* and 2 teaspoons *vanilla*.

Chocolate-Topped Almond Fingers

2¾ cups all-purpose flour
¼ teaspoon baking soda
1 cup butter *or* margarine
1 cup sugar
1 egg
2 tablespoons milk
1 teaspoon vanilla
½ cup finely chopped almonds, toasted
⅓ cup semisweet chocolate pieces
1 tablespoon shortening
¼ cup Amaretto
1 to 1¼ cups sifted powdered sugar
Finely chopped almonds, toasted (optional)

In a medium mixing bowl stir together flour and baking soda (see photo 1, page 14). Set aside.

In a large mixer bowl beat butter or margarine with an electric mixer on medium speed for 30 seconds. Add sugar and beat till fluffy (see photo 1, page 31). Add egg, milk, and vanilla and beat well. Gradually stir or beat in flour mixture till combined (see photo 1, page 42). Stir in the ½ cup almonds. If necessary, cover and chill about 1 hour or till easy to handle.

Roll rounded teaspoons of dough into 2-inch ropes (see photo 2, page 43). Place ropes 1½ inches apart on an ungreased cookie sheet. Bake in a 375° oven for 6 to 8 minutes or till edges are firm and bottoms are lightly browned (see photo 3, page 43). Remove and cool completely on wire racks (see photo 4, page 31).

In a small heavy saucepan melt chocolate and shortening over low heat, stirring constantly. Stir in Amaretto and enough powdered sugar to make of drizzling consistency. Drizzle melted chocolate mixture over cookies. (If mixture thickens while drizzling, stir in hot *water*, a few drops at a time.) Sprinkle with additional finely chopped almonds, if desired. Makes about 60.

Molasses-Spice Cookies

You'll be amazed how fast these spicy, chewy treats disappear.

2¼ **cups all-purpose flour**
 2 **teaspoons baking soda**
 1 **teaspoon ground ginger**
 ½ **teaspoon ground allspice *or*
    ground cinnamon**
 ¼ **teaspoon ground mace *or* ground cloves**
 ¾ **cup shortening**
 1 **cup packed brown sugar**
 1 **egg**
 ¼ **cup molasses**
 1 **teaspoon finely shredded lemon peel
    (optional)**
   Sugar

In a large mixing bowl stir together flour, baking soda, ginger, allspice or cinnamon, and mace or cloves (see photo 1, page 14). Set aside.

In a large mixer bowl beat shortening with an electric mixer on medium speed for 30 seconds. Add brown sugar and beat till fluffy (see photo 1, page 31). Add the egg, molasses, and lemon peel, if desired, and beat well. Gradually stir or beat in the flour mixture till combined (see photo 1, page 42).

Shape dough into 1¼-inch balls (see photo 2, page 43). Place sugar in a pie plate or shallow bowl. Roll balls in sugar to coat. Place balls 2 inches apart on an ungreased cookie sheet.

Bake in a 375° oven for 8 to 10 minutes or till edges are firm and bottoms are lightly browned (see photo 3, page 43). Cool on cookie sheet for 1 minute. Remove and cool completely on wire racks (see photo 4, page 31). Makes about 48.

Peppered Pfeffernuesse

Saying Peppered Pfeffernuesse (FEF-uhr-noos) is fun, but not as much fun as eating these spicy German Christmas cookies that typically contain pepper.

 ⅓ **cup molasses**
 ¼ **cup butter *or* margarine**
 2 **cups all-purpose flour**
 ¼ **cup packed brown sugar**
 ¾ **teaspoon ground cinnamon**
 ½ **teaspoon baking soda**
 ½ **teaspoon aniseed, crushed**
 ¼ **teaspoon ground cardamom**
 ¼ **teaspoon ground allspice**
   Dash pepper
 1 **beaten egg**
 2 **tablespoons finely chopped candied
    citron (optional)**
   Sifted powdered sugar

In a large saucepan combine molasses and butter or margarine. Heat and stir over low heat till butter or margarine melts. Remove from heat. Cool to room temperature.

Meanwhile, in a large mixing bowl stir together flour, brown sugar, cinnamon, baking soda, aniseed, cardamom, allspice, and pepper (see photo 1, page 14). Set aside.

Stir egg into cooled molasses mixture. Gradually stir in flour mixture till combined (see photo 1, page 42). Stir in citron, if desired. If necessary, transfer dough to a bowl and cover and chill about 1 hour or till easy to handle.

Grease a cookie sheet. Set aside. Shape dough into 1¼-inch balls (see photo 2, page 43). Place 1 inch apart on prepared cookie sheet. Bake in a 350° oven for 10 to 12 minutes or till edges are firm and bottoms are lightly browned (see photo 3, page 43). Remove and cool completely on wire racks (see photo 4, page 31). Roll in powdered sugar to coat. Makes about 36.

Make-a-Cookie Mix

Batter up! The next time your favorite slugger touches home base, have a batch of cookies waiting. It's fast and easy with our homemade mix.

These cookies start with a basic mix you can keep on hand for months.

Choose Cranberry Drops, Great Cocoa Bars, or decorative Gumdrop Cookies. No matter which recipe you pick, you're sure to bat a thousand with the home team.

Gumdrop Cookies

49

Make-a-Cookie Mix

*Store this handy homemade mix in the freezer for 6
months or on the shelf for 6 weeks.*

4	cups all-purpose flour
1	cup sugar
1	cup packed brown sugar
2	teaspoons baking powder
1½	cups shortening that does not require refrigeration

In a large mixing bowl stir together flour, sugar,
brown sugar, and baking powder (see photo 1,
page 14). Cut in shortening till mixture resembles fine crumbs (see photo 1). Store tightly
covered at room temperature for up to 6 weeks.

To measure, lightly spoon mix into a measuring
cup and level with a spatula (see photo 2).
Makes about 8½ cups.

1 Use a pastry blender
to work the shorten-
ing into the flour mix-
ture till it's cut up into
fine crumbs, as shown.
Be sure to use solid
shortening that doesn't
require refrigeration,
not cooking oil or melt-
ed butter.

Gumdrop Cookies

½	cup gumdrops
3	cups Make-a-Cookie Mix
1	slightly beaten egg
1	teaspoon vanilla
	Sugar
	Gumdrops (optional)

Finely chop the ½ cup gumdrops (see photo 3).
In a large mixing bowl stir together gumdrops,
Make-a-Cookie Mix, egg, and vanilla. Shape
dough into 1½-inch balls (see photo 2, page
43). Place balls 2 inches apart on an ungreased
cookie sheet. Flatten slightly with the bottom of
a glass dipped in sugar. Cut decorative shapes
from additional gumdrops and press lightly into
cookies, if desired.

Bake in a 375° oven for 8 to 10 minutes or till
bottoms are lightly browned (see photo 3, page
43). Remove and cool completely on wire racks
(see photo 4, page 31). Makes about 24.

2 To measure dry ingredients such as the Make-a-Cookie Mix, use a dry measuring cup exactly the size you need. Spoon the mix lightly into the cup, then level it off with a metal spatula or the flat side of a knife.

3 On a cutting board, use a sharp knife to finely chop the gumdrops. If the knife gets sticky, dip the blade into cold water. *Or,* try snipping the gumdrops into small pieces with kitchen scissors.

Great Cocoa Bars

Moist and mouth-watering, these quick-to-fix bars make an irresistible chocolate treat.

2½ cups Make-a-Cookie Mix
¼ cup sugar
¼ cup unsweetened cocoa powder
1 slightly beaten egg
½ cup milk
½ cup miniature semisweet chocolate pieces
½ cup chopped nuts
Powdered sugar

Grease a 9x9x2-inch baking pan. Set aside. In a large mixing bowl stir together Make-a-Cookie Mix, sugar, and cocoa powder. In a small mixing bowl stir together egg and milk. Stir into dry ingredients, along with chocolate pieces and nuts. Spread batter evenly into prepared pan (see photo 3, page 15).

Bake in a 350° oven for 25 to 30 minutes or till a wooden toothpick inserted in center comes out clean (see photo 4, page 15). Cool completely on a wire rack. Sift powdered sugar over cookies. Cut into bars (see photo 5, page 15). Makes 24.

Raisin Bars

2¾ cups Make-a-Cookie Mix
1 cup raisins
⅓ cup applesauce
2 slightly beaten eggs
1 tablespoon milk
1 teaspoon vanilla
¼ teaspoon ground cinnamon
¼ teaspoon ground nutmeg
Spice Frosting
Ground nutmeg

Grease a 9x9x2-inch baking pan. Set aside. In a medium mixing bowl stir together Make-a-Cookie Mix, raisins, applesauce, eggs, milk, vanilla, cinnamon, and nutmeg. Mix well.

Spread batter evenly into prepared pan (see photo 3, page 15). Bake in a 350° oven about 25 minutes or till a wooden toothpick inserted in center comes out clean (see photo 4, page 15). Cool completely on a wire rack. Frost with Spice Frosting. Sprinkle with nutmeg. Cut into bars (see photo 5, page 15). Makes 36.

Spice Frosting: In a small mixer bowl beat together 1½ cups sifted *powdered sugar;* 3 tablespoons *butter or margarine,* softened; and ¼ teaspoon ground *cinnamon.* Add enough *milk* (1 to 2 tablespoons) to make spreadable.

◄ *Pictured opposite: Raisin Bars*

Cranberry Drops

3 cups Make-a-Cookie Mix
½ teaspoon ground nutmeg
1 slightly beaten egg
2 tablespoons orange juice
1½ cups finely chopped cranberries
    (2 cups unchopped)
½ cup chopped walnuts

In a large mixing bowl stir together Make-a-Cookie Mix and nutmeg. Stir in egg and orange juice. Mix well. Stir in cranberries and nuts.

Drop by rounded teaspoons 2 inches apart onto an ungreased cookie sheet (see photo 2, page 31). Bake in a 350° oven about 20 minutes or till bottoms are lightly browned (see photo 3, page 31). Remove and cool completely on wire racks (see photo 4, page 31). Makes about 42.

Oatmeal-Peanut Cookies

2½ cups Make-a-Cookie Mix
¼ cup packed brown sugar
2 slightly beaten eggs
½ cup milk
½ teaspoon vanilla
1 cup quick-cooking rolled oats
1 cup chopped peanuts

In a large mixing bowl stir together Make-a-Cookie Mix, brown sugar, eggs, milk, and vanilla. Mix well. Stir in oats and peanuts.

Drop by rounded teaspoons 2 inches apart onto an ungreased cookie sheet (see photo 2, page 31). Bake in a 375° oven for 8 to 10 minutes or till bottoms are lightly browned (see photo 3, page 31). Remove and cool completely on wire racks (see photo 4, page 31). Makes about 42.

All About Cookie Sheets

Cookie sheets are more than just trays that hold dollops of cookie dough while the chips melt. They affect the color, shape, and texture of your baked cookies.
● When you're shopping for a cookie sheet, look for a shiny, heavy-gauge aluminum one with very low sides or no sides at all.
● Avoid dark cookie sheets because they absorb heat and may cause overbrowning on the bottoms of cookies. Nonstick cookie sheets work well if they're not too dark.
● Keep the size of your oven in mind, too: there should be 1 to 2 inches between the sheet and the oven walls and door to allow for good air circulation. And even if your oven is small, don't put one sheet directly over another one. This also results in poor air circulation within the oven.
● Grease cookie sheets only when the recipe recommends it. Otherwise, cookies may spread too much.
● Nonstick sheets sometimes cause a slight variance in cookie texture. Because liquids bead up on nonstick surfaces, the cookie batter doesn't spread quite as much. The baked results are a little thicker, with very smooth bottoms.

Banana Chippers

Keep these cookies in the freezer to store them longer than one day.

3 cups Make-a-Cookie Mix
⅓ cup mashed banana
1 slightly beaten egg
½ teaspoon vanilla
½ cup miniature semisweet
    chocolate pieces

In a large mixing bowl stir together Make-a-Cookie Mix, banana, egg, and vanilla. Mix well. Stir in chocolate pieces.

Drop by rounded teaspoons 2 inches apart onto an ungreased cookie sheet (see photo 2, page 31). Bake in a 375° oven about 10 minutes or till bottoms are lightly browned (see photo 3, page 31). Remove and cool completely on wire racks (see photo 4, page 31). Makes about 36.

Carrot Cookies

How can you make these soft, drop cookies even better? Try topping them with the Cream Cheese Frosting on page 17.

2½ cups Make-a-Cookie Mix
1 cup finely shredded carrot
¼ cup toasted wheat germ
½ teaspoon finely shredded orange peel
1 slightly beaten egg
2 tablespoons milk
½ teaspoon vanilla

Stir together Make-a-Cookie Mix, carrot, wheat germ, and orange peel. Combine egg, milk, and vanilla. Stir into carrot mixture, mixing well.

Drop by rounded teaspoons 2 inches apart onto an ungreased cookie sheet (see photo 2, page 31). Bake in a 375° oven for 8 to 10 minutes or till bottoms are lightly browned (see photo 3, page 31). Remove and cool completely on wire racks (see photo 4, page 31). Makes about 30.

Jam Gems

These yummy cookies puff high as they bake and flatten out again as they cool.

2 cups Make-a-Cookie Mix
1 slightly beaten egg yolk
2 tablespoons milk
1 teaspoon finely shredded lemon peel
1 teaspoon vanilla
1 slightly beaten egg white
¾ cup finely chopped walnuts
2 tablespoons desired jam *or* jelly

Grease a cookie sheet. Set aside. In a medium mixing bowl stir together Make-a-Cookie Mix, egg yolk, milk, lemon peel, and vanilla. Cover and chill about 30 minutes or till easy to handle.

Shape dough into 1¼-inch balls (see photo 2, page 43). Roll each ball in the beaten egg white, then in the nuts. Place 2 inches apart on prepared cookie sheet. Press down centers with a moistened finger.

Bake in a 350° oven for 14 to 15 minutes or till bottoms are lightly browned (see photo 3, page 43). Remove and cool completely on wire racks (see photo 4, page 31). Spoon about ¼ teaspoon jam or jelly into the center of *each* cookie. Store overnight in the refrigerator or freeze for longer storage. Makes about 24.

Roped Delights

At the end of your rope trying to decide what kind of cookie to make? We've got the answer to your dilemma all tied up.

Citrus Kringla or Cinnamon Candy Cane Cookies will add a new twist to any cookie jar.

Meander through this chapter and enjoy the twists and turns of every cookie. One nibble and you'll be roped into baking these cookies for family and friends.

Spicy Wheat Wreaths

57

Spicy Wheat Wreaths

1	cup all-purpose flour
¼	teaspoon baking powder
½	cup whole wheat flour
½	teaspoon ground cinnamon
¼	teaspoon ground ginger
	Dash ground cloves
¾	cup butter *or* margarine
¾	cup sugar
1	egg
1	teaspoon vanilla
½	cup all-purpose flour
12	red *or* green candied cherries, halved

Combine the 1 cup all-purpose flour and baking powder (see photo 1, page 14). Set aside. Combine whole wheat flour, cinnamon, ginger, and cloves (see photo 1, page 14). Set aside.

In a large mixer bowl beat butter or margarine with an electric mixer on medium speed for 30 seconds. Add sugar and beat till fluffy (see photo 1, page 31). Add egg and vanilla; beat well. Gradually add flour-baking powder mixture, beating till combined. Divide dough in half.

Add whole wheat flour mixture to one half, stirring till combined. Add the ½ cup all-purpose flour to the other half, stirring till combined. Cover each half and chill about 30 minutes or till easy to handle.

On a lightly floured surface roll *each* half into a 12-inch log (see photo 1). Cut *each* log into *twenty-four* ½-inch pieces (see photo 2). Roll each piece into a 6-inch rope. Place a white and a brown rope side by side and twist together about 6 times (see photo 3). Shape twisted ropes into a circle, gently pinching where ends meet (see photo 4). Place 2 inches apart on an ungreased cookie sheet. Place *1* cherry half over the spot where the ends meet on *each* wreath.

Bake in a 375° oven for 8 to 10 minutes or till edges are firm and bottoms are lightly browned (see photo 3, page 43). Cool on cookie sheet for 1 minute. Remove and cool completely on wire racks (see photo 4, page 31). Makes 24.

1 Shape the dough into a log by working it with your hands and rolling it on a lightly floured counter till it measures the correct length. Lay a ruler down next to the log so the size is easy to check.

2 Using a sharp, thin-bladed knife, cut the log into the correct number of pieces. Use the ruler again to make sure each piece is the size called for in the recipe.

3 Roll each small piece of dough into a thin rope. Place a white rope and a brown rope side by side and twist several times.

4 Bring the two rope ends together to form a circle. Gently pinch the ends together where they meet.

Citrus Kringla

The soft dough of these Norwegian favorites bakes into a tender, cakelike cookie.

 3 **cups all-purpose flour**
2½ **teaspoons baking powder**
 1 **teaspoon baking soda**
 ½ **cup butter *or* margarine**
 1 **cup sugar**
 1 **egg**
1½ **teaspoons finely shredded lemon peel *or* orange peel**
 ¾ **cup buttermilk**

In a medium mixing bowl stir together flour, baking powder, and baking soda (see photo 1, page 14). Set aside.

In a large mixer bowl beat butter or margarine with an electric mixer on medium speed for 30 seconds. Add sugar and beat till fluffy (see photo 1, page 31). Add egg and lemon peel or orange peel and beat well. Add flour mixture and buttermilk alternately to beaten mixture, beating till combined. Cover and chill for 4 hours or overnight or till easy to handle.

Divide dough in half. (Return one half to the refrigerator till you're ready to work with it.) On a lightly floured surface roll each half into a 10x5-inch rectangle. Cut each rectangle crosswise into twenty 5x½-inch strips. Roll each strip into a 10-inch rope (see photo 3, page 59).

On an ungreased cookie sheet shape each rope into a loop, crossing 1½ inches from ends. Twist rope at crossing point. Lift ends over to loop and seal, forming a pretzel shape.

Bake in a 425° oven about 5 minutes or till edges are firm and bottoms are lightly browned, though tops will be pale (see photo 3, page 43). Remove and cool completely on wire racks (see photo 4, page 31). Makes 40.

Cinnamon Candy Cane Cookies

Cover the dough you're not working with and place it in the refrigerator so it doesn't dry out.

1¾ **cups all-purpose flour**
 ½ **teaspoon baking powder**
 ⅓ **cup shortening**
 ⅓ **cup butter *or* margarine**
 ⅔ **cup sugar**
 1 **egg**
 1 **teaspoon vanilla**
 2 **drops oil of cinnamon**
 4 **to 6 drops red food coloring**

In a small bowl stir together flour and baking powder (see photo 1, page 14). Set aside.

In a large mixer bowl beat shortening and butter or margarine with an electric mixer on medium speed for 30 seconds. Add sugar and beat till fluffy (see photo 1, page 31). Add egg, vanilla, and oil of cinnamon and beat well. Gradually add flour mixture, beating till combined. Divide dough in half. Stir food coloring into one half. Cover each half and chill about 30 minutes or till easy to handle.

Divide each color of dough in half. On a lightly floured surface roll each portion of dough into a 9-inch log (see photo 1, page 58). Cut *each* log into *eighteen* ½-inch pieces (see photo 2, page 58). Roll each piece into a 4-inch rope. Place a red and a white rope side by side and twist together (see photo 3, page 59). Pinch ends to seal (see photo 4, page 59). Form twisted ropes into a cane. Place 2 inches apart on an ungreased cookie sheet.

Bake in a 375° oven for 8 to 10 minutes or till edges are firm and bottoms are lightly browned (see photo 3, page 43). Remove and cool completely on wire racks (see photo 4, page 31). Makes 36.

Flaky Dutch Letters

2½ cups almonds, finely ground
⅔ cup sifted powdered sugar
2 egg whites
1 teaspoon vanilla
1½ cups butter *or* margarine
3 cups all-purpose flour
¼ cup ice water
1 egg yolk

For filling, in a small mixer bowl beat together ground almonds, powdered sugar, egg whites, and vanilla. Cover and chill thoroughly.

For dough, in a large mixing bowl cut butter or margarine into flour till mixture resembles coarse crumbs (see photo 1, page 50). Sprinkle *1 tablespoon* ice water over part of the mixture. Gently toss with a fork and push to the side of the bowl. Repeat with remaining ice water till all is moistened. Form into a ball. Cover and let stand about 10 minutes or till easy to handle.

On a lightly floured surface roll dough into a 10x12-inch rectangle. Fold into thirds. Repeat rolling and folding twice. Divide dough into thirds. Cover and set aside. With moistened hands, roll the filling into two 7½-inch logs (see photo 1, page 58). Cut logs into 1-inch pieces (see photo 2, page 58), combining the two ½-inch pieces from the ends of both logs. Roll each piece of filling into a 7½-inch rope (see photo 3, page 59). You'll have a total of 15.

On a lightly floured surface roll each third of dough into an 8x10-inch rectangle. Cut into five 8x2-inch strips. Place 1 filling rope on each strip of dough. Wrap dough around filling. Seal edges and ends. Shape into "S" shapes. Place 2 inches apart on an ungreased cookie sheet.

In a small mixing bowl combine egg yolk and 1 tablespoon *water*. Brush on letters. Bake in a 375° oven for 30 to 35 minutes or till golden. Remove and cool completely on wire racks (see photo 4, page 31). To store for more than 1 day, wrap and freeze. Makes 15.

Decorated Berliner Kranzer

These buttery, wreath-shaped Scandinavian favorites literally melt in your mouth.

1 cup butter *or* margarine
½ cup sifted powdered sugar
1 hard-cooked egg yolk, sieved
1 raw egg yolk
¼ teaspoon almond extract
2¼ cups all-purpose flour
1 slightly beaten egg white
6 to 8 sugar cubes, crushed
   Chopped red *or* green candied cherries (optional)

In a large mixer bowl beat butter or margarine with an electric mixer on medium speed for 30 seconds. Add powdered sugar and beat till fluffy (see photo 1, page 31). Add both egg yolks and almond extract and beat well. Gradually stir in flour till combined. Cover and chill about 1 hour or till easy to handle.

Divide dough in half. Roll each half into a 9-inch log (see photo 1, page 58). Cut *each* log into *eighteen* ½-inch pieces (see photo 2, page 58). Roll each piece into a 6-inch rope (see photo 3, page 59). Shape each rope into a ring, overlapping about 1 inch from ends. Brush with egg white and sprinkle with crushed sugar cubes. If desired, press a few pieces of chopped candied cherries into the cookie at the point where the ropes overlap. Place 2 inches apart on an ungreased cookie sheet.

Bake in a 350° oven about 10 minutes or till edges are firm and bottoms are lightly browned (see photo 3, page 43). Remove and cool completely on wire racks (see photo 4, page 31). Makes 36.

Tasty Cookie Tarts

Here's our candidate for "Cookie Most Likely To Succeed"—whether it's for teatime or lunchtime or for family or guests.

Each rich, flaky pastry shell is not only a cookie base, but also a delightful, edible container for a delectable filling.

So next time you vote for best cookie, cast your ballot for these tiny cookie tarts. They're a winner in every category.

Mini Cheesecake Tarts

Mini Cheesecake Tarts

Keep these melt-in-your-mouth morsels on hand in your freezer—they're ideal for spur-of-the-moment entertaining. Dollop each with jelly just before serving.

1	**cup all-purpose flour**
⅓	**cup sugar**
¼	**cup unsweetened cocoa powder**
½	**cup butter *or* margarine**
2	**to 3 tablespoons water**
2	**3-ounce packages cream cheese, softened**
¼	**cup sugar**
2	**tablespoons milk**
1	**teaspoon vanilla**
1	**egg**
	Jelly, jam, *or* marmalade (optional)

For pastry, in a small mixing bowl stir together flour, the ⅓ cup sugar, and cocoa powder. Cut in butter or margarine till pieces are the size of small peas (see photo 2, page 22). Sprinkle with water, 1 tablespoon at a time, tossing gently till all is moistened (photo 1).

Form dough into a ball. Divide dough into 24 balls. Place each ball in an ungreased 1¾-inch muffin cup. Press dough evenly against bottom and sides of cup (see photo 2).

For filling, in a small mixer bowl beat cream cheese and the ¼ cup sugar till fluffy. Beat in milk and vanilla. Add egg and beat at low speed just till combined. Fill *each* pastry-lined muffin cup with about *1 tablespoon* of the cream cheese filling (see photo 3).

Bake in a 325° oven for 15 to 18 minutes or till done. Cool for 30 minutes in pans. Remove from pans and cool completely on wire racks (see photo 4). Top each tart with jelly, jam, or marmalade, if desired. Makes 24.

1 Sprinkle 1 tablespoon water over part of the flour mixture. Gently toss with a fork. Push to the side of the bowl and repeat with remaining water till all the mixture is moistened.

2 Press the dough *evenly* against the bottoms and sides of the muffin cups. If the dough is too thin at any one place, the tarts may crack as they bake and allow the filling to leak through.

3 Use a measuring spoon to divide the filling mixture evenly among the muffin cups.

4 It's easier to remove the tarts after baking if you let them cool slightly in the muffin pans first. Then, carefully lift the tarts out with a metal spatula and let them finish cooling on wire racks.

Rocky Road Tarts

½ cup butter *or* margarine, softened
1 3-ounce package cream cheese, softened
1 cup all-purpose flour
¼ cup ground walnuts, pecans, *or* almonds
1 8-ounce bar milk chocolate, cut up
1 cup tiny marshmallows
⅓ cup coarsely chopped walnuts, pecans, *or* almonds

For pastry, in a small mixer bowl beat together butter or margarine and cream cheese. Add flour and ground nuts, stirring till combined. Cover and chill dough about 1 hour or till easy to handle.

Divide dough into 24 balls. Place each ball in an ungreased 1¾-inch muffin cup. Press dough evenly against bottom and sides of cup (see photo 2, page 64). Bake in a 325° oven for 20 to 22 minutes or till done. Cool slightly in pan.

Meanwhile, for filling, in a small heavy saucepan melt chocolate over low heat, stirring constantly. Remove saucepan from heat. Stir in marshmallows and chopped nuts.

Quickly fill *each* pastry-lined muffin cup with about *1 rounded teaspoon* of filling (see photo 3, page 65). Chill till center is firm. Remove from pans (see photo 4, page 65). Let stand at room temperature about 20 minutes before serving. Makes 24.

Fruited Sesame Tassies

Toasted sesame seed add a rich, nutty flavor to these bite-size tidbits.

1 6-ounce package (1½ cups) mixed dried fruit bits
1½ cups water
½ cup orange marmalade
1 tablespoon toasted sesame seed
½ cup butter *or* margarine
¼ cup packed brown sugar
2 tablespoons water
1½ cups all-purpose flour
⅓ cup quick-cooking rolled oats

For filling, in a small saucepan combine dried fruit and the 1½ cups water. Bring to boiling. Reduce heat and simmer, covered, for 8 minutes or till fruit is very tender. Drain. Stir marmalade and sesame seed into fruit. Set aside.

For pastry, in a small mixer bowl beat butter or margarine on medium speed of an electric mixer for 30 seconds. Add brown sugar and beat till fluffy (see photo 1, page 31). Beat in the 2 tablespoons water. Add flour and oats, stirring till combined.

Divide dough into 36 balls. Place each ball in an ungreased 1¾-inch muffin cup. Press dough evenly against bottom and sides of cup (see photo 2, page 64). Fill *each* pastry-lined muffin cup with about *1 tablespoon* of the filling (see photo 3, page 65).

Bake in a 325° oven for 28 to 30 minutes or till done. Cool for 5 minutes in pans. Remove from pans and cool completely on wire racks (see photo 4, page 65). Makes 36.

Fudgy Liqueur Cups

As one editor put it, "They're like eating fudge in a chocolate shell."

¾ **cup all-purpose flour**
¼ **cup unsweetened cocoa powder**
⅓ **cup butter *or* margarine, softened**
⅓ **cup sugar**
1 **3-ounce package cream cheese, softened**
¼ **cup butter *or* margarine**
½ **cup sugar**
⅓ **cup unsweetened cocoa powder**
1 **egg**
2 **tablespoons Grand Marnier, Cointreau, *or* cherry liqueur**
1 **teaspoon vanilla**

For pastry, in a small mixing bowl stir together flour and the ¼ cup cocoa powder. Set aside. In a small mixer bowl beat the ⅓ cup butter or margarine, the ⅓ cup sugar, and cream cheese till fluffy. Gradually add flour mixture, beating till combined. If necessary, cover and chill dough about 30 minutes or till easy to handle.

Divide dough into 24 balls. Place each ball in a lightly greased 1¾-inch muffin cup. Press dough evenly against bottom and sides of cup (see photo 2, page 64).

For filling, in a small saucepan melt the ¼ cup butter or margarine over low heat. Remove from heat and stir in the ½ cup sugar; the ⅓ cup cocoa powder; egg; Grand Marnier, Cointreau, or cherry liqueur; and vanilla. Fill *each* pastry-lined muffin cup with about *1 tablespoon* filling (see photo 3, page 65).

Bake in a 325° oven about 18 minutes or till filling is set. Cool for 10 minutes in pans. Remove from pans and cool completely on wire racks (see photo 4, page 65). Makes 24.

Bonbon Bites

½ **of a 4-ounce package German sweet chocolate**
⅓ **cup butter *or* margarine, softened**
1 **3-ounce package cream cheese, softened**
1 **cup all-purpose flour**
¼ **cup apricot preserves, seedless raspberry preserves, *or* cherry preserves**
½ **of a 1-ounce square semisweet chocolate**
1 **tablespoon butter *or* margarine**
½ **cup sifted powdered sugar**
¼ **teaspoon vanilla**
1 **tablespoon boiling water**

For pastry, in a small heavy saucepan melt German sweet chocolate over low heat, stirring often. Remove saucepan from heat and cool slightly. In a small mixer bowl beat together the ⅓ cup butter or margarine, cream cheese, and melted chocolate. Gradually add flour, beating till combined. Cover and chill dough about 1 hour or till easy to handle.

Divide dough into 24 balls. Place each ball in an ungreased 1¾-inch muffin cup. Press dough evenly against bottom and sides of cup (see photo 2, page 64).

Bake in a 350° oven for 15 to 18 minutes or till done. Cool slightly in pans. Remove from pans and cool completely on wire racks (see photo 4, page 65). Fill *each* pastry-lined muffin cup with about ½ *teaspoon* desired preserves (see photo 3, page 65).

In a small heavy saucepan melt semisweet chocolate and the 1 tablespoon butter or margarine over low heat, stirring often. Remove saucepan from heat and add powdered sugar and vanilla, stirring till crumbly. Stir in water till smooth. (Add more *water*, a few drops at a time, if necessary, to make of drizzling consistency.) Drizzle a little of the chocolate mixture over each tart. Chill till chocolate drizzle is firm. Makes 24.

Cookie Cutouts

The sky's the limit! Let your imagination soar when you make a batch of these cookie cutouts.

One try at this cookie-making method and you'll have earned your wings. Roll out the dough, then cut into shapes—any shape you like.

Our selection of high-in-the-sky flavors gives you everything you need to successfully land a crew of cookie lovers.

High-in-the-Sky Cookie Pops

High-in-the-Sky Cookie Pops

2¾ **cups all-purpose flour**
1 **teaspoon baking soda**
⅓ **cup butter *or* margarine**
¼ **cup sugar**
1 **egg**
⅔ **cup honey**
½ **teaspoon lemon extract *or* vanilla**
Wooden sticks
1 **egg yolk**
1 **teaspoon water**
Food coloring

In a medium mixing bowl stir together flour and baking soda (see photo 1, page 14). Set aside.

In a large mixer bowl beat butter or margarine with an electric mixer on medium speed for 30 seconds. Add sugar and beat till fluffy (see photo 1, page 31). Add egg, honey, and lemon extract or vanilla and beat well. Gradually add flour mixture, beating till combined. Divide dough into thirds. Cover and chill about 1 hour or till easy to handle. Meanwhile, cut moon, rainbow, and cloud shapes out of cardboard.

Grease a cookie sheet. Set aside. On a lightly floured surface roll dough ¼ inch thick (see photo 1). Use a sharp knife to cut around cardboard patterns (see photo 2). For star shapes, use a cookie cutter. Place 1 inch apart on prepared cookie sheet. Tuck a wooden stick under the center of each cookie. Press dough around stick to secure (see photo 3).

In a small bowl beat together egg yolk and water. Divide mixture between 3 or 4 small bowls. Add 2 or 3 drops of a different food coloring to each bowl and mix well. Paint cookies to look like moons, rainbows, clouds, and stars (see photo 4). (If colored yolk mixture thickens while standing, stir in *water,* a drop at a time.)

Bake in a 350° oven for 6 to 8 minutes or till edges are firm and bottoms are very lightly browned (see photo 3, page 43). Remove and cool completely on wire racks (see photo 4, page 31). Makes about 30.

1 Using a floured rolling pin, roll the cookie dough out on a lightly floured surface, such as a countertop or pastry cloth. Roll to the thickness specified in the recipe. Use a ruler to be sure that all the dough is the same thickness for even baking.

2 Cut the dough into shapes using floured cookie cutters, or create your own cardboard patterns, as shown. Make cutouts as close together as possible. Reroll scraps to cut more cookies.

3 Tuck a wooden stick under the center of each cookie. Press the dough down so the cookie bakes around the stick.

4 Use a clean small paintbrush to paint each unbaked cookie with the colored egg yolk and water mixture.

Scottish Shortbread

1¼ **cups all-purpose flour**
 3 **tablespoons sugar**
 ½ **cup butter *or* margarine**

In a medium mixing bowl stir together flour and sugar. Cut in butter or margarine till mixture resembles fine crumbs (see photo 1, page 50). Form mixture into a ball and knead till smooth.

For wedges, on an ungreased cookie sheet roll dough into an 8-inch circle. Using your fingers, press to make a scalloped edge. With a fork, prick dough deeply to make 16 pie-shaped wedges. Bake in a 300° oven for 40 to 45 minutes or till center is set and edges are very lightly browned. Cut along perforations while warm.

For strips or rounds, on a lightly floured surface roll dough slightly more than ¼ inch thick (see photo 1, page 70). Cut into 24 (2x1-inch) strips with a knife or into 24 rounds with a 1½-inch cookie cutter (see photo 2, page 71). Place 1 inch apart on an ungreased cookie sheet. Bake in a 300° oven for 20 to 25 minutes or till edges are firm and bottoms are lightly browned (see photo 3, page 43). Remove and cool completely on wire racks (see photo 4, page 31). Makes 16 wedges or 24 strips or rounds.

Cocoa Shortbread: Prepare Scottish Shortbread as above, *except* add 2 tablespoons *unsweetened cocoa powder* with the flour.

Cinnamon Shortbread: Prepare Scottish Shortbread as above, *except* after cutting in butter or margarine, sprinkle mixture with 10 drops *oil of cinnamon* (about ⅛ teaspoon) and knead till smooth.

Orange-Ginger Shortbread: Prepare Scottish Shortbread as above, *except* stir ¼ teaspoon ground *ginger* into flour mixture and add 1 teaspoon finely shredded *orange peel* with the butter or margarine.

Whole Wheat Joe Froggers

Legend has it that Uncle Joe was an old man who made great molasses cookies. The cookies were named Joe Froggers because they were as big and dark as the frogs hopping around Uncle Joe's pond.

2½ **cups all-purpose flour**
1½ **cups whole wheat flour**
1½ **teaspoons ground ginger**
 ½ **teaspoon baking soda**
 ½ **teaspoon ground cloves**
 ½ **teaspoon ground cinnamon**
 ⅛ **teaspoon ground mace**
 ¾ **cup butter *or* margarine**
 1 **cup packed brown sugar**
 ¾ **cup molasses**
 ¼ **cup milk**

In a large mixing bowl stir together all-purpose flour, whole wheat flour, ginger, baking soda, cloves, cinnamon, and mace (see photo 1, page 14). Set aside.

In a large mixer bowl beat butter or margarine with an electric mixer on medium speed for 30 seconds. Add brown sugar and beat till fluffy (see photo 1, page 31). Stir together molasses and milk. Add flour mixture and molasses mixture alternately to beaten mixture, beating till combined. Cover and chill for several hours or overnight or till easy to handle.

Grease a cookie sheet. Set aside. On a well-floured surface roll dough ¼ inch thick (see photo 1, page 70). Cut with a 4-inch-round cookie cutter (see photo 2, page 71). Place 1 inch apart on prepared cookie sheet. Bake in a 350° oven for 10 to 12 minutes or till edges are firm and bottoms are very lightly browned (see photo 3, page 43). Cool on cookie sheet for 1 minute. Remove and cool completely on wire racks (see photo 4, page 31). Makes about 20.

Chocolate Cutouts

Planning to keep these cookies around for more than a couple of days? We discovered they store better in an airtight container in the freezer.

  2 **squares (2 ounces) semisweet chocolate**
1¾ **cups all-purpose flour**
1½ **teaspoons baking powder**
  ¼ **cup shortening**
  ¼ **cup butter *or* margarine**
  ¾ **cup packed brown sugar**
  1 **egg**
  1 **tablespoon milk**
  ¼ **teaspoon coconut flavoring**
      ***or* almond extract**
      Powdered sugar

In a small heavy saucepan melt chocolate over low heat, stirring often. Remove saucepan from heat and cool.

In a small bowl stir together flour and baking powder (see photo 1, page 14). Set aside.

In a large mixer bowl beat shortening and butter or margarine with an electric mixer on medium speed for 30 seconds. Add brown sugar and beat till fluffy (see photo 1, page 31). Add melted chocolate, egg, milk, and coconut flavoring or almond extract and beat well. Gradually add flour mixture, beating till combined. Divide dough in half. Cover and chill about 3 hours or till easy to handle.

On a lightly floured surface roll dough ⅛ inch thick (see photo 1, page 70). Cut into desired shapes with 2-inch cookie cutters (see photo 2, page 71). Place 1 inch apart on an ungreased cookie sheet. Bake in a 375° oven for 6 to 8 minutes or till edges are firm and bottoms are very lightly browned (see photo 3, page 43). Cool on cookie sheet for 1 minute. Remove and cool completely on wire racks (see photo 4, page 31). Sift powdered sugar over cookies. Makes about 60.

Cookies and Corn Oil Margarine

When you're making cookies, the firmness of the dough varies, depending on whether you use butter, margarine, or margarine that's made from 100 percent corn oil. The latter makes cookie dough so soft that you'll need to change the chilling times given in our cookie recipes or the chilling temperature.

If you use 100 percent corn oil margarine in cutout cookies, extend the chilling time to 5 hours before you roll out the dough. For slice and bake cookies, chill the rolls of dough in the freezer rather than in the refrigerator.

Products labeled "spreads" and "diet" aren't recommended for cookie making. Neither are soft-style tub products.

Spicy Cream Cheese Cookies

Try mixing a little allspice or nutmeg in with the sugar that's sprinkled over the tops of these soft sugar cookies.

4½ **cups all-purpose flour**
2 **teaspoons baking powder**
1 **teaspoon baking soda**
½ **teaspoon ground allspice** *or*
   ground nutmeg
1 **cup butter** *or* **margarine**
1 **3-ounce package cream cheese,**
   softened
1 **cup sugar**
1 **cup packed brown sugar**
2 **eggs**
1 **teaspoon finely shredded lemon peel**
1 **teaspoon vanilla**
¼ **cup buttermilk** *or* **sour milk***
   Sugar

In a medium mixing bowl stir together flour, baking powder, baking soda, and allspice or nutmeg (see photo 1, page 14). Set aside.

In a large mixer bowl beat butter or margarine and cream cheese with an electric mixer on medium speed for 30 seconds. Add sugar and brown sugar and beat till fluffy (see photo 1, page 31). Add eggs, lemon peel, and vanilla and beat well. Add flour mixture and buttermilk or sour milk alternately to beaten mixture, beating till combined. Divide dough in half. Cover and chill about 3 hours or till easy to handle.

On a lightly floured surface roll dough ⅜ inch thick (see photo 1, page 70). Cut with 2- or 3-inch cookie cutters (see photo 2, page 71). Place 2½ inches apart on an ungreased cookie sheet. Sprinkle lightly with additional sugar. Bake in a 350° oven for 10 to 12 minutes or till edges are firm and bottoms are very lightly browned (see photo 3, page 43). Remove and cool completely on wire racks (see photo 4, page 31). Makes 54 to 78.

*Note: To make sour milk, combine 1½ teaspoons *lemon juice or vinegar* and enough *milk* to make ½ cup. Let stand for 5 minutes.

German Honey Cakes

Aging this spicy variation of the rich German cookie, Lebkuchen, lets the flavors mellow and allows the cookie to soften a bit.

3 **cups all-purpose flour**
1 **tablespoon pumpkin pie spice**
½ **teaspoon baking soda**
1 **egg**
¾ **cup packed brown sugar**
1 **teaspoon finely shredded lemon peel**
½ **cup honey**
½ **cup dark molasses**
½ **cup slivered almonds**
½ **cup chopped candied citron**
1½ **cups sifted powdered sugar**
2 **tablespoons water**

In a medium mixing bowl stir together flour, pumpkin pie spice, and baking soda (see photo 1, page 14). Set aside.

In a large mixer bowl beat egg. Add brown sugar and lemon peel and beat till fluffy. Stir in honey and molasses. Gradually add flour mixture, beating till combined. Stir in almonds and citron. Divide dough in half. Cover and chill for several hours or overnight or till easy to handle.

Grease a cookie sheet. Set aside. On a well-floured surface roll dough into a 14x7-inch rectangle (about ¼ inch thick) (see photo 1, page 70). Cut into 3½x2-inch rectangles. Place 2 inches apart on prepared cookie sheet. Bake in a 375° oven for 8 to 10 minutes or till edges are firm and bottoms are very lightly browned (see photo 3, page 43). Cool on cookie sheet for 1 minute. Remove and cool slightly on wire racks (see photo 4, page 31).

Meanwhile, for glaze, in a small mixing bowl combine powdered sugar and water. Mix well. Brush glaze over cookies while still warm. Store in an airtight container for 3 days before serving. Makes 28.

Gingerbread People

1¾ cups all-purpose flour
¾ cup whole wheat flour
¾ teaspoon baking soda
½ teaspoon ground ginger
½ teaspoon ground cinnamon
¼ teaspoon ground allspice
¼ teaspoon ground nutmeg
½ cup shortening
½ cup packed brown sugar
1 egg
⅓ cup molasses
3 tablespoons honey
1 tablespoon lemon juice
2 cups sifted powdered sugar
1 egg white
2 teaspoons lemon juice
  Food coloring (optional)
  Decorative candies (optional)

In a medium mixing bowl stir together flours, baking soda, ginger, cinnamon, allspice, and nutmeg (see photo 1, page 14). Set aside.

Beat shortening for 30 seconds. Add brown sugar; beat till fluffy (see photo 1, page 31). Add egg, molasses, honey, and the 1 tablespoon lemon juice; beat well. Gradually add flour mixture, beating till combined. (You may have to stir in the last part of the flour mixture with a wooden spoon.) Divide dough in half. Cover and chill about 3 hours or till easy to handle.

Grease a cookie sheet. Set aside. On a floured surface roll dough ⅛ inch thick (see photo 1, page 70). Cut with 3- to 4-inch people cookie cutters (see photo 2, page 71). Place 1 inch apart on prepared cookie sheet. Bake in a 375° oven for 4 to 5 minutes or till edges are firm and bottoms are lightly browned (see photo 3, page 43). Cool for 1 minute. Remove and cool completely on wire racks (see photo 4, page 31).

For frosting, beat together powdered sugar, egg white, and the 2 teaspoons lemon juice. If desired, stir several drops of food coloring into frosting to tint. Spread frosting over cookies. If desired, decorate with candies. Makes about 54.

Decorated Sugar Cookies

2 cups all-purpose flour
1½ teaspoons baking powder
⅓ cup butter *or* margarine
⅓ cup shortening
1½ cups sifted powdered sugar
1 egg
1 tablespoon milk
½ teaspoon vanilla
3 cups sifted powdered sugar
3 tablespoons milk
½ teaspoon vanilla
  Food coloring (optional)
  Colored sugar (optional)

In a medium bowl stir together flour and baking powder (see photo 1, page 14). Set aside.

In a large mixer bowl beat butter or margarine and shortening with an electric mixer on medium speed for 30 seconds. Add the 1½ cups powdered sugar and beat till fluffy (see photo 1, page 31). Add egg, the 1 tablespoon milk, and ½ teaspoon vanilla and beat well. Gradually add flour mixture, beating till combined. Divide dough in half. Cover and chill about 3 hours or till easy to handle.

On a lightly floured surface roll dough ⅛ inch thick (see photo 1, page 70). Use a sharp knife to cut around cardboard patterns or cut with 2-inch cookie cutters (see photo 2, page 71). Place 1 inch apart on an ungreased cookie sheet. Bake in a 375° oven for 7 to 8 minutes or till edges are firm and bottoms are very lightly browned (see photo 3, page 43). Remove and cool on wire racks (see photo 4, page 31).

For frosting, combine the 3 cups powdered sugar, the 3 tablespoons milk, and ½ teaspoon vanilla. (If desired, stir a few drops of food coloring into all or part of the frosting to tint.) Spread frosting over cookies. *Or,* fill a decorating bag no more than half full of frosting. (Add 2 to 4 tablespoons additional powdered sugar for piping). Using any tip with a small opening, pipe on outlines or names. *Or,* if desired, sprinkle frosted cookies with colored sugar. Makes about 56.

Slice 'n' Bake

For a cookie wish list that includes piping hot cookies that bake in minutes, this chapter commands results.

No magic wands or silly spells are needed here. These sliced cookies, also called refrigerator cookies, give you a head start on baking. Just roll the dough into logs and chill till you're ready to slice and bake.

Then, keep the dough handy and bake up a batch of irresistible homemade cookies for unexpected guests, after-school snacks, or a halftime break for sports fans.

*Grasshopper Cookie
Sandwiches*

Grasshopper Cookie Sandwiches

You can make the frosting for these sandwich cookies with white crème de menthe, too. For color, simply add a few drops of green food coloring.

2	**cups all-purpose flour**
½	**cup unsweetened cocoa powder**
½	**teaspoon baking soda**
½	**cup butter *or* margarine**
½	**cup shortening**
1	**cup sugar**
1	**egg**
3	**tablespoons crème de menthe**
	Grasshopper Frosting

In a medium mixing bowl stir together flour, cocoa powder, and baking soda (see photo 1, page 14). Set aside.

In a large mixer bowl beat butter or margarine and shortening with an electric mixer on medium speed for 30 seconds. Add sugar and beat till fluffy (see photo 1, page 31). Add egg and crème de menthe and beat well. Gradually add the flour mixture, beating till combined. Cover and chill about 45 minutes or till easy to handle (see photo 1).

On waxed paper or clear plastic wrap, shape dough into two 7-inch rolls. Wrap and chill for several hours or overnight. (If using corn oil margarine, chill in the freezer for 1 to 2 hours or till dough is firm enough to slice.) Remove 1 roll from the refrigerator.

Unwrap and reshape slightly if necessary, then carefully cut dough into ⅛-inch slices (see photo 2). Place 1 inch apart on an ungreased cookie sheet (see photo 3). Bake in a 375° oven for 6 to 8 minutes or till edges are firm and dough has a dull appearance (see photo 3, page 43). Remove and cool completely on wire racks (see photo 4, page 31). Repeat with remaining dough.

Frost the bottoms of *half* of the cookies with Grasshopper Frosting (see photo 4). Top *each* with a remaining unfrosted cookie, bottom side down. Makes about 54.

Grasshopper Frosting: In a large mixer bowl beat ⅓ cup *butter or margarine* with an electric mixer on medium speed for 30 seconds. Gradually add 2 cups sifted *powdered sugar,* beating well. Beat in ¼ cup green *crème de menthe.* Gradually beat in 1½ cups sifted *powdered sugar.* If necessary, add additional green *crème de menthe* to make frosting spreadable.

1 Cover the mixer bowl tightly with clear plastic wrap or foil. Place the cookie dough in the refrigerator to chill till it's firm enough to handle and shape.

2 Before slicing, check to see if the roll has flattened out on the bottom during chilling. If necessary, reshape the roll by gently rolling it on the cutting board. Slice the dough cross-wise. Keep rotating the roll as you slice to avoid flattening one side.

3 Use a pancake turner or wide metal spatula to arrange the cookies about 1 inch apart on a cookie sheet.

4 Spread a generous amount of frosting on the bottoms of *half* of the cookies. Press a frosted and an un-frosted cookie together sandwich-style.

Whole Wheat-Peanut Slices

1½ **cups all-purpose flour**
1 **cup whole wheat flour**
½ **teaspoon baking soda**
½ **cup butter *or* margarine**
½ **cup shortening**
½ **cup sugar**
½ **cup packed brown sugar**
1 **egg**
½ **teaspoon vanilla**
1 **cup finely chopped peanuts**

In a medium mixing bowl stir together all-purpose flour, whole wheat flour, and baking soda (see photo 1, page 14). Set aside.

In a large mixer bowl beat butter or margarine and shortening with an electric mixer on medium speed for 30 seconds. Add sugar and brown sugar and beat till fluffy (see photo 1, page 31). Add egg and vanilla and beat well. Gradually add flour mixture, beating till combined. Cover and chill about 45 minutes or till easy to handle (see photo 1, page 78).

On waxed paper or clear plastic wrap, shape dough into two 7-inch rolls. Roll in peanuts to coat. Wrap and chill several hours or overnight. (If using corn oil margarine, chill in the freezer for 1 to 2 hours or till dough is firm enough to slice.) Remove 1 roll from the refrigerator.

Unwrap and reshape slightly if necessary, then carefully cut dough into ¼-inch slices (see photo 2, page 79). Place 1 inch apart on an ungreased cookie sheet (see photo 3, page 79).

Bake in a 375° oven for 8 to 10 minutes or till edges are firm and bottoms are lightly browned (see photo 3, page 43). Remove and cool completely on wire racks (see photo 4, page 31). Repeat with remaining dough. Makes about 54.

Buttery Almond Slices

Chop the toasted almonds into very tiny pieces—you'll find the cookie rolls easier to slice.

2⅓ **cups all-purpose flour**
1 **teaspoon baking powder**
¾ **cup butter *or* margarine**
1 **cup sugar**
1 **egg**
1 **tablespoon milk**
¼ **teaspoon almond extract**
1 **cup toasted almonds, finely chopped**

In a medium bowl stir together flour and baking powder (see photo 1, page 14). Set aside.

In a large mixer bowl beat butter or margarine with an electric mixer on medium speed for 30 seconds. Add sugar; beat till fluffy (see photo 1, page 31). Add egg, milk, and almond extract and beat well. Gradually add flour mixture, beating till combined. Cover and chill about 45 minutes or till easy to handle (see photo 1, page 78).

On waxed paper or clear plastic wrap, shape dough into two 7-inch rolls. Roll in almonds to coat. Wrap and chill several hours or overnight. (If using corn oil margarine, chill in the freezer for 1 to 2 hours or till dough is firm enough to slice). Remove 1 roll from the refrigerator.

Unwrap and reshape slightly if necessary, then carefully cut dough into ¼-inch slices (see photo 2, page 79). Place 1 inch apart on an ungreased cookie sheet (see photo 3, page 79).

Bake in a 375° oven for 8 to 10 minutes or till edges are firm and bottoms are lightly browned (see photo 3, page 43). Remove and cool completely on wire racks (see photo 4, page 31). Repeat with remaining dough. Makes about 54.

Molasses-Date Sliced Cookies

Beat in the dates with an electric mixer to distribute them evenly.

2 **cups all-purpose flour**
½ **teaspoon baking powder**
½ **cup butter *or* margarine**
½ **cup packed brown sugar**
¼ **cup sugar**
1 **egg**
¼ **cup molasses**
2 **teaspoons vanilla**
1 **cup pitted whole dates,
    finely chopped**

In a medium bowl stir together flour and baking powder (see photo 1, page 14). Set aside.

In a large mixer bowl beat butter or margarine with an electric mixer on medium speed for 30 seconds. Add brown sugar and sugar and beat till fluffy (see photo 1, page 31). Add egg, molasses, and vanilla and beat well. Gradually add flour mixture, beating till combined. Beat in dates just till combined. Cover and chill dough about 45 minutes or till easy to handle (see photo 1, page 78).

On waxed paper or clear plastic wrap, shape dough into two 7-inch rolls. Wrap and chill for several hours or overnight. (If using corn oil margarine, chill in the freezer about 4 hours or till dough is firm enough to slice.) Grease a cookie sheet. Set aside. Remove 1 roll from the refrigerator.

Unwrap and reshape slightly if necessary, then carefully cut dough into ¼-inch slices (see photo 2, page 79). Place 1 inch apart on the prepared cookie sheet (see photo 3, page 79).

Bake in a 375° oven for 8 to 10 minutes or till edges are firm and bottoms are lightly browned (see photo 3, page 43). Remove and cool completely on wire racks (see photo 4, page 31). Repeat with remaining dough. Makes about 54.

Cardamom-Lemon Refrigerator Cookies

2¼ **cups all-purpose flour**
1½ **teaspoons baking powder**
1 **teaspoon ground cardamom**
½ **cup butter *or* margarine**
½ **cup shortening**
1 **cup sugar**
1 **egg**
1 **teaspoon finely shredded lemon peel**
½ **cup finely chopped nuts**

In a medium mixing bowl stir together flour, baking powder, and cardamom (see photo 1, page 14). Set aside.

In a large mixer bowl beat butter or margarine and shortening with an electric mixer on medium speed for 30 seconds. Add sugar and beat till fluffy (see photo 1, page 31). Add egg and lemon peel and beat well. Gradually add flour mixture, beating till combined. Stir in nuts. Cover and chill about 45 minutes or till easy to handle (see photo 1, page 78).

On waxed paper or clear plastic wrap, shape dough into two 7-inch rolls. Wrap and chill for several hours or overnight. (If using corn oil margarine, chill in the freezer for 1 to 2 hours or till dough is firm enough to slice.) Remove 1 roll from the refrigerator.

Unwrap and reshape slightly if necessary, then carefully cut dough into ¼-inch slices (see photo 2, page 79). Place 1 inch apart on an ungreased cookie sheet (see photo 3, page 79).

Bake in a 375° oven for 8 to 10 minutes or till edges are firm and bottoms are lightly browned (see photo 3, page 43). Remove and cool completely on wire racks (see photo 4, page 31). Repeat with remaining dough. Makes about 54.

Filled Cookie Pockets

A pleasant surprise always brings a big smile— especially if the surprise is a hidden treasure. You'll be all smiles as you bite into one of these sweet and delicious treats.

Each cookie is stuffed with a load of sweet jams, bits of fruit, or chips of brickle and butterscotch.

For safekeeping, we suggest you store the cookies in a secret place, because once hungry pirates smell the aroma of these gems, they're sure to raid the cookie jar.

Sugar and Spice Rounds

Sugar and Spice Rounds

1½ **cups all-purpose flour**
½ **teaspoon baking soda**
½ **teaspoon ground cinnamon**
½ **teaspoon ground ginger**
½ **teaspoon ground nutmeg**
⅛ **teaspoon ground cloves**
½ **cup butter *or* margarine**
½ **cup sugar**
1 **egg**
1 **teaspoon finely shredded orange peel**
1 **teaspoon vanilla**
½ **cup raisins, chopped**
½ **cup finely chopped nuts**
3 **tablespoons orange marmalade**

In a medium mixing bowl stir together flour, soda, cinnamon, ginger, nutmeg, and cloves (see photo 1, page 14). Set aside.

In a large mixer bowl beat butter or margarine with an electric mixer on medium speed for 30 seconds. Add sugar and beat till fluffy (see photo 1, page 31). Add egg, orange peel, and vanilla and beat well. Gradually add flour mixture, beating till combined.

Cover and chill about 1 hour or till easy to handle (see photo 1, page 78). Meanwhile, for filling, in a small mixing bowl stir together raisins, nuts, and marmalade.

On a lightly floured surface roll dough ⅛ inch thick (see photo 1, page 70). Cut into rounds with a 2½-inch cookie cutter (see photo 2, page 71). Place some of the cutout rounds 1 inch apart on an ungreased cookie sheet (see photo 3, page 79). Spoon about *2 rounded teaspoons* of filling onto the center of *each* round (see photo 1). Top with remaining rounds (see photo 2). Seal edges (see photo 3).

Bake in a 350° oven for 8 to 10 minutes or till edges are firm and bottoms are lightly browned (see photo 3, page 43). Remove and cool completely on wire racks (see photo 4, page 31). Makes about 20.

1 Transfer some of the cutout cookie rounds to an ungreased cookie sheet. Spoon filling onto the center of each cookie.

2 Lay one of the remaining dough rounds over each cookie on the cookie sheet.

3 Lightly seal the edges by pressing the two cutout cookies together with the tines of a fork. *Or,* make a scalloped design in the dough by sealing the edges together with the tip of a spoon.

Overstuffed Pockets

Expect these apple-butter-stuffed sugar cookies to soften up a bit as they're stored.

2 cups all-purpose flour
¼ cup toasted wheat germ
½ teaspoon baking powder
½ cup butter *or* margarine
⅓ cup shortening
⅔ cup sugar
1 egg
1 teaspoon vanilla
¾ cup apple butter

In a medium mixing bowl stir together flour, wheat germ, and baking powder (see photo 1, page 14). Set aside.

In a large mixer bowl beat butter or margarine and shortening with an electric mixer on medium speed for 30 seconds. Add sugar and beat till fluffy (see photo 1, page 31). Add egg and vanilla and beat well. Gradually add flour mixture, beating till combined. Cover and chill about 1 hour or till easy to handle (see photo 1, page 78).

Grease a cookie sheet. Set aside. On a lightly floured surface roll dough ⅛ inch thick (see photo 1, page 70). Cut into rounds with a 2-inch cookie cutter (see photo 2, page 71). Place some of the cutout rounds on the prepared cookie sheet (see photo 3, page 79). Spoon about *1 teaspoon* of apple butter onto center of *each* round (see photo 1, page 84). Top with remaining rounds (see photo 2, page 85). Seal edges (see photo 3, page 85).

Bake in a 350° oven about 10 minutes or till edges are firm and bottoms are lightly browned (see photo 3, page 43). Remove and cool completely on wire racks (see photo 4, page 31). Makes about 36.

Fruity Pillows

3½ cups all-purpose flour
2 teaspoons baking powder
½ teaspoon baking soda
1 cup shortening
¾ cup sugar
¾ cup packed brown sugar
2 eggs
1 teaspoon vanilla
About 1 cup desired jam, preserves, canned pie filling, *or* cake and pastry filling

In a large mixing bowl stir together flour, baking powder, and baking soda (see photo 1, page 14). Set aside.

In a large mixer bowl beat shortening with an electric mixer on medium speed for 30 seconds. Add sugar and brown sugar and beat till fluffy (see photo 1, page 31). Add eggs and vanilla and beat well. Gradually add flour mixture, beating till combined. Cover and chill about 1 hour or till easy to handle (see photo 1, page 78).

Grease a cookie sheet. Set aside. On a lightly floured surface roll dough ⅛ inch thick (see photo 1, page 70). Cut into 2-inch squares (see photo 2, page 71). Place some of the cutout squares 1 inch apart on the prepared cookie sheet (see photo 3, page 79). Spoon about *1 teaspoon* jam onto the center of *each* square (see photo 1, page 84). Top with remaining squares (see photo 2, page 85). Seal edges (see photo 3, page 85).

Bake in a 350° oven for 9 to 10 minutes or till edges are firm and bottoms are lightly browned (see photo 3, page 43). Remove and cool completely on wire racks (see photo 4, page 31). Makes about 48.

Butterscotch-Stuffed Cocoa Cookies

Doll up these stuffed triangles by drizzling a little Powdered Sugar Glaze (see recipe, page 99) over the tops.

2 **cups all-purpose flour**
⅓ **cup unsweetened cocoa powder**
1½ **teaspoons baking powder**
⅔ **cup butter *or* margarine**
¾ **cup sugar**
1 **egg**
1 **tablespoon milk**
1 **teaspoon vanilla**
½ **cup butterscotch-flavored pieces**
½ **cup almond brickle pieces**

In a medium mixing bowl stir together flour, cocoa powder, and baking powder (see photo 1, page 14). Set aside.

In a mixer bowl beat butter or margarine with an electric mixer on medium speed for 30 seconds. Add sugar and beat till fluffy (see photo 1, page 31). Add egg, milk, and vanilla and beat well. Gradually add flour mixture, beating till combined. Divide dough in half. Cover and chill about 1 hour or till easy to handle (see photo 1, page 78). Meanwhile, for filling, in a small mixing bowl combine butterscotch-flavored pieces and almond brickle pieces.

Grease a cookie sheet. Set aside. On a lightly floured surface roll dough ⅛ inch thick (see photo 1, page 70). Cut into 2-inch squares (see photo 2, page 71). Place some of the cutout squares 1 inch apart on the prepared cookie sheet (see photo 3, page 79). Spoon about ½ *teaspoon* filling onto center of *each* square (see photo 1, page 84). Fold dough diagonally over filling into a triangle. Seal edges (see photo 3, page 85).

Bake in a 350° oven about 8 minutes or till edges are firm and bottoms are lightly browned (see photo 3, page 43). Remove and cool completely on wire racks (see photo 4, page 31). Makes about 60.

Gingerbread Gems

2½ **cups all-purpose flour**
1 **teaspoon ground ginger**
¾ **teaspoon baking soda**
½ **teaspoon ground cinnamon**
½ **teaspoon ground cloves**
½ **cup shortening**
½ **cup sugar**
1 **egg**
⅓ **cup molasses**
½ **of an 8-ounce package cream cheese, softened**
1 **egg yolk**
2 **tablespoons sugar**
1½ **teaspoons vanilla**
Powdered Sugar

Stir together flour, ginger, soda, cinnamon, and cloves (see photo 1, page 14). Set aside.

In a large mixer bowl beat shortening with an electric mixer on medium speed for 30 seconds. Add the ½ cup sugar and beat till fluffy (see photo 1, page 31). Add the whole egg and molasses and beat well. Gradually add flour mixture, beating till combined. (You may have to stir in the last part of the flour mixture with a wooden spoon.) Divide dough in half. Cover and chill about 1 hour or till easy to handle (see photo 1, page 78). Meanwhile, for filling, stir together cream cheese, egg yolk, the 2 tablespoons sugar, and vanilla.

Grease a cookie sheet. Set aside. On a lightly floured surface roll dough ⅛ inch thick (see photo 1, page 70). Cut into rounds with a 3-inch cookie cutter (see photo 2, page 71). Place some of the cutout rounds 1 inch apart on the prepared cookie sheet (see photo 3, page 79). Spoon a scant *1 teaspoon* filling onto the center of *each* round (see photo 1, page 84). Fold in half. Seal edges (see photo 3, page 85).

Bake in a 350° oven about 10 minutes or till edges are firm and bottoms are lightly browned (see photo 3, page 43). Remove and cool completely on wire racks (see photo 4, page 31). Sift powdered sugar over cookies. Makes about 36.

Perfect Pinwheels

Round and round and round they go and where they stop nobody knows.

But don't worry about this delicious dilemma—one bite will solve it. In cookie pinwheels, you'll find two tempting flavors and textures that whirl and twirl together. One is a rich dough, and the other, a gooey filling.

The results: crispy cookie wheels with a double dose of flavor.

*Pistachio
Pinwheels*

Pistachio Pinwheels

2	cups all-purpose flour
½	teaspoon baking powder
½	cup butter *or* margarine
¼	cup shortening
1	cup sugar
3	tablespoons milk
1	teaspoon vanilla
1½	teaspoons finely shredded lemon peel
2	tablespoons sugar
2	teaspoons cornstarch
2	tablespoons lemon juice
1½	cups pistachio nuts, chopped

In a mixing bowl stir together flour and baking powder (see photo 1, page 14). Set aside. Beat butter and shortening with an electric mixer for 30 seconds. Add the 1 cup sugar; beat till fluffy (see photo 1, page 31). Add milk, vanilla, and ½ *teaspoon* lemon peel; beat well. Gradually add *half* the flour mixture, beating till combined. Stir in remaining flour mixture. Cover; chill 1 hour or till easy to handle (see photo 1, page 78).

Meanwhile, for filling, in a saucepan combine the 2 tablespoons sugar and cornstarch. Stir in lemon juice, remaining lemon peel, and ⅓ cup *water*. Cook and stir till thickened and bubbly, then cook and stir for 2 minutes more. Stir in nuts. Remove from heat. Cool for 10 minutes.

On a floured surface roll dough into a 16x12-inch rectangle (see photo 1). Spread filling to within ½ inch of edges (see photo 2). Roll up, jelly-roll style, starting from one of the long sides (see photo 3). Pinch to seal. Cut roll in half crosswise. Wrap and chill. (If using corn oil margarine, chill in the freezer for 1 to 2 hours or till firm enough to slice.) Grease a cookie sheet. Set aside. Remove 1 roll from refrigerator. Unwrap and reshape if necessary. Carefully cut dough into ¼-inch slices (see photo 4). Place on prepared cookie sheet (see photo 3, page 79).

Bake in a 375° oven for 10 to 12 minutes or till edges are firm and bottoms are lightly browned (see photo 3, page 43). Remove; cool completely (see photo 4, page 31). Makes about 60.

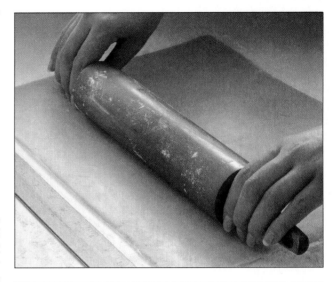

1 Place the dough on a lightly floured countertop or pastry cloth. Flatten it slightly and smooth the edges with your hands. Using a floured rolling pin, roll from the center to the edges with light, even strokes, forming a rectangle. Reshape into a rectangle with your hands as you work.

2 Use a metal spatula to spread the filling over the dough. Leave about a ½-inch-wide border around all four sides of the rectangle. That way, the filling won't seep out as you roll up the dough.

3 Carefully roll up the dough rectangle, starting from one of the long sides. Pinch the dough together to seal firmly. Cut the long roll in half crosswise so it's easier to handle.

4 Cut the dough rolls crosswise into ¼-inch slices using a sharp, thin-bladed knife. Place a ruler beside each roll to make sure all of the cookies you cut are the same size.

Cranberry-Orange Twirls

1	10-ounce package frozen cranberry-orange relish, thawed
1	teaspoon cornstarch
2½	cups all-purpose flour
½	teaspoon baking soda
1	cup butter *or* margarine
1	cup sugar
1	egg
¼	teaspoon almond extract (optional)

For filling, in a small saucepan combine cranberry-orange relish and cornstarch. Cook and stir over medium heat till thickened and bubbly, then cook and stir for 1 minute more. Cool. In a medium mixing bowl stir together flour and baking soda (see photo 1, page 14). Set aside.

In a large mixer bowl beat butter or margarine with an electric mixer on medium speed for 30 seconds. Add sugar and beat till fluffy (see photo 1, page 31). Add egg and almond extract, if desired, and beat well. Gradually add flour mixture, beating till combined. Cover and chill for 1 to 2 hours or till easy to handle (see photo 1, page 78).

On a floured surface roll dough into a 16x12-inch rectangle (see photo 1, page 90). Spread filling to within ½ inch of edges (see photo 2, page 90). Roll up, jelly-roll style, starting from one of the long sides (see photo 3, page 91). Pinch to seal. Cut roll in half crosswise. Wrap in waxed paper or clear plastic wrap and chill for several hours or overnight. (If using corn oil margarine, chill in the freezer for 1 to 2 hours or till firm enough to slice.)

Grease a cookie sheet. Set aside. Remove 1 roll from the refrigerator. Unwrap and reshape slightly if necessary. Carefully cut dough into ¼-inch slices (see photo 4, page 91). Place 2 inches apart on prepared cookie sheet (see photo 3, page 79). Bake in a 375° oven for 10 to 12 minutes or till edges are firm and bottoms are lightly browned (see photo 3, page 43). Remove and cool completely on wire racks (see photo 4, page 31). Makes about 60.

Apricot-Nut Swirls

½	cup finely snipped dried apricots
½	cup water
¼	cup packed brown sugar
¼	cup finely chopped walnuts
1¼	cups all-purpose flour
½	cup whole wheat flour
½	teaspoon baking soda
½	cup butter *or* margarine
½	cup sugar
1	egg

For filling, in a small saucepan stir together apricots and water. Simmer, covered, about 15 minutes or till water is nearly absorbed and apricots are tender. Cool, then mash slightly. Stir in brown sugar and nuts. Set aside.

In a medium mixing bowl stir together all-purpose flour, whole wheat flour, and baking soda (see photo 1, page 14). In a large mixer bowl beat butter or margarine on medium speed of an electric mixer for 30 seconds. Add sugar and beat till combined. Beat in egg. Gradually add flour mixture, beating till combined.

On a floured surface roll dough into a 12x10-inch rectangle (see photo 1, page 90). Spread filling to within ½ inch of edges (see photo 2, page 90). Roll up, jelly-roll style, starting from one of the long sides (see photo 3, page 91). Pinch to seal. Cut roll in half crosswise. Wrap in waxed paper or clear plastic wrap and chill for several hours or overnight. (If using corn oil margarine, chill in the freezer for 1 to 2 hours or till firm enough to slice.)

Grease a cookie sheet. Set aside. Remove 1 roll from the refrigerator. Unwrap and reshape slightly if necessary. Carefully cut dough into ¼-inch slices (see photo 4, page 91). Place 2 inches apart on prepared cookie sheet (see photo 3, page 79). Bake in a 375° oven for 8 to 10 minutes or till edges are firm and bottoms are lightly browned (see photo 3, page 43). Cool on cookie sheet for 1 minute. Remove and cool completely on wire racks (see photo 4, page 31). Makes about 36.

Choco-Peanut Butter Cookie Roll

Surround a chocolate center with peanut butter cookie dough and you've captured an all-time favorite flavor.

1⅓ **cups all-purpose flour**
½ **teaspoon baking soda**
½ **cup creamy peanut butter**
¼ **cup butter *or* margarine**
½ **cup sugar**
½ **cup packed brown sugar**
1 **egg**
2 **tablespoons milk**
1 **teaspoon vanilla**
1 **6-ounce package (1 cup) semisweet chocolate pieces**
2 **tablespoons butter *or* margarine**

In a medium mixing bowl stir together flour and baking soda (see photo 1, page 14). Set aside.

In a large mixer bowl beat peanut butter and the ¼ cup butter or margarine on medium speed of an electric mixer for 30 seconds. Add sugar and brown sugar and beat till fluffy (see photo 1, page 31). Add egg, milk, and vanilla; beat well. Gradually add flour mixture, beating till combined. Reserve *two-thirds* of dough. Set aside.

In a small heavy saucepan melt chocolate and the 2 tablespoons butter or margarine over low heat, stirring often. Stir chocolate mixture into the remaining *one-third* of the dough. Mix well.

Roll peanut butter dough into a 10x12-inch rectangle between 2 sheets of waxed paper (see photo 1, page 90). Peel off top sheet of waxed paper. Roll chocolate dough into a 10x12-inch rectangle between 2 sheets of waxed paper (see photo 1, page 90). Peel off top sheet of waxed paper. Carefully invert chocolate rectangle over peanut butter rectangle. Peel off waxed paper. Roll up, jelly-roll style, starting from one of the long sides (see photo 3, page 91). Pinch to seal. Cut roll in half crosswise. Wrap in waxed paper or clear plastic wrap and chill for several hours or overnight. (If using corn oil margarine, chill in the freezer for 1 to 2 hours or till dough is firm enough to slice.)

Remove 1 roll from the refrigerator. Unwrap and reshape slightly if necessary. Carefully cut dough into ¼-inch slices (see photo 4, page 91). Place 2 inches apart on an ungreased cookie sheet (see photo 3, page 79).

Bake in a 375° oven about 8 minutes or till edges are firm and bottoms are lightly browned (see photo 3, page 43). Cool on cookie sheet for 1 minute. Remove and cool completely on wire racks (see photo 4, page 31). Makes about 48.

Fancy Pressed Cookies

Appearances can be deceiving. This array of cookies is surprisingly simple to create.

No sleight of hand required here. Simply use a cookie press to transform ordinary dough into extraordinarily rich, buttery confections.

So, for an afternoon tea or a ballroom bash, add a spark of magic with these fancy pressed treats.

Double-Peanut Spritz

Double-Peanut Spritz

½ cup all-purpose flour
½ cup whole wheat flour
¼ teaspoon baking soda
½ cup peanut butter
¼ cup butter *or* margarine
½ cup sugar
½ cup packed brown sugar
1 egg
2 squares (2 ounces) semisweet chocolate
2 teaspoons shortening
½ cup chopped peanuts

In a small mixing bowl stir together all-purpose flour, whole wheat flour, and baking soda (see photo 1, page 14). Set aside.

In a large mixer bowl beat peanut butter and butter or margarine with an electric mixer on medium speed for 30 seconds. Add sugar and brown sugar and beat till fluffy (see photo 1, page 31). Add egg and beat well. Gradually add the flour mixture, beating till combined. Do not chill dough.

Pack dough into a cookie press (see photo 1). Using the ribbon plate (or desired design plate), force dough through the cookie press onto an ungreased cookie sheet (see photo 2). Bake in a 400° oven for 5 to 7 minutes or till edges are firm but not brown. Remove and cool completely on wire racks (see photo 4, page 31).

Meanwhile, in a small heavy saucepan melt chocolate and shortening over low heat, stirring often. Dip half of each cookie into chocolate, then peanuts (see photo 3). Makes about 48.

1 Before you fill the manual or electric cookie press, pick the design plate you want to use and put it in place following the cookie press directions. Then pack the cookie dough into the tube.

2 For ribbon cookies, hold the cookie press at an angle, as shown. For other cookie shapes, hold the cookie press straight up and down. Press out enough dough so that it sticks to the cookie sheet but not so much that it squeezes out from under the press. Stop pressing out dough before you lift the press off the cookies.

3 Dip half of each cooled cookie into the chocolate. Immediately dip the chocolate-covered ends of the cookies into a bowl of chopped peanuts.

Spritz

For a truly festive cookie, divide the dough into thirds and tint each a different color. Pack all three colored doughs side by side into the cookie press and watch what happens!

3½ **cups all-purpose flour**
1 **teaspoon baking powder**
1½ **cups butter *or* margarine**
1 **cup sugar**
1 **egg**
1 **teaspoon vanilla**
½ **teaspoon lemon *or* orange extract, *or***
    ¼ **teaspoon almond *or* mint extract**
Food coloring (optional)
Colored sugar *or*
    decorative candies (optional)

In a medium bowl combine flour and baking powder (see photo 1, page 14). Set aside.

In a large mixer bowl beat butter or margarine with an electric mixer on medium speed for 30 seconds. Add sugar and beat till fluffy (see photo 1, page 31). Add egg, vanilla, and flavored extract and beat well. Gradually add flour mixture, beating till combined. If desired, tint dough with food coloring. Do not chill dough.

Pack dough into a cookie press (see photo 1, page 96). Force dough through the cookie press onto an ungreased cookie sheet (see photo 2, page 97). Decorate with colored sugar or candies, if desired.

Bake in a 400° oven for 6 to 8 minutes or till edges are firm but not brown. Remove and cool completely on wire racks (see photo 4, page 31). Makes about 60.

Nutty Spritz

These rich, buttery cookies are like snowflakes: No two are shaped exactly alike.

2½ **cups all-purpose flour**
1 **cup finely ground walnuts *or* pecans**
1 **teaspoon baking powder**
1 **cup butter *or* margarine**
½ **cup sugar**
½ **cup packed brown sugar**
1 **egg**
1 **teaspoon vanilla**
Powdered sugar (optional)

In a large mixing bowl stir together flour, ground nuts, and baking powder (see photo 1, page 14). Set aside.

In a large mixer bowl beat butter or margarine on medium speed of an electric mixer for 30 seconds. Add sugar and brown sugar and beat till fluffy (see photo 1, page 31). Add egg and vanilla and beat well. Gradually add flour mixture, beating till combined. Do not chill dough.

Pack dough into a cookie press (see photo 1, page 96). Force dough through the cookie press onto an ungreased cookie sheet (see photo 2, page 97).

Bake in a 400° oven for 6 to 8 minutes or till edges are firm but not brown. Cool on cookie sheet for 1 minute. Remove and cool completely on wire racks (see photo 4, page 31). Sift powdered sugar over cookies, if desired. Makes about 60.

Pressed Gingerbread Cookies

These molasses and spice cookies have a cakier texture than traditional Spritz.

2¾ **cups all-purpose flour**
¾ **teaspoon baking powder**
½ **teaspoon ground nutmeg**
½ **teaspoon ground cinnamon**
¼ **teaspoon ground cloves**
¼ **teaspoon ground ginger**
1 **cup butter *or* margarine**
¼ **cup molasses**
¼ **cup packed brown sugar**
1 **egg**
1 **teaspoon vanilla**
  Powdered Sugar Glaze (optional)

In a large mixing bowl stir together flour, baking powder, nutmeg, cinnamon, cloves, and ginger (see photo 1, page 14). Set aside.

In a large mixer bowl beat butter or margarine on medium speed of an electric mixer for 30 seconds. Add molasses and brown sugar and beat till combined. Add egg and vanilla and beat well. Gradually stir in flour mixture till combined. Do not chill dough.

Pack dough into a cookie press (see photo 1, page 96). Force dough through the cookie press onto an ungreased cookie sheet (see photo 2, page 97). Bake in a 400° oven for 6 to 8 minutes or till edges are firm but not brown. Remove and cool completely on wire racks (see photo 4, page 31). If desired, drizzle cookies with Powdered Sugar Glaze. Makes about 48.

Powdered Sugar Glaze: In a small mixing bowl combine 1 cup sifted *powdered sugar,* ¼ teaspoon *vanilla,* and enough *milk* to make of drizzling consistency (about 1½ tablespoons).

Coconut-Cocoa Spritz

3⅓ **cups all-purpose flour**
1 **cup coconut, finely chopped**
3 **tablespoons unsweetened cocoa powder**
1 **teaspoon baking powder**
1½ **cups butter *or* margarine**
1¼ **cups sugar**
1 **egg**
1 **teaspoon vanilla**

In a large mixing bowl stir together flour, coconut, cocoa powder, and baking powder (see photo 1, page 14). Set aside.

In a large mixer bowl beat butter or margarine on medium speed of an electric mixer for 30 seconds. Add sugar and beat till fluffy (see photo 1, page 31). Add egg and vanilla and beat well. Gradually add flour mixture, beating till combined. Do not chill dough.

Pack dough into a cookie press (see photo 1, page 96). Force dough through the cookie press onto an ungreased cookie sheet (see photo 2, page 97).

Bake in a 400° oven for 6 to 8 minutes or till edges are firm but not brown. Remove and cool completely on wire racks (see photo 4, page 31). Makes about 80.

Meringues And Macaroons

Mmmm good! That's the perfect description for these marvelous meringues and macaroons.

Egg whites give both of these cookies their one-of-a-kind characteristics.

Meringue cookies boast a light and fluffy texture with a delicate crispness. Macaroons are airy cookies with a chewy, coconut goodness.

Munch one morsel of these cookies, and you'll be asking for more!

Meringue Snowmen

Meringue Snowmen

Fun to make, delightful to eat.

2	**egg whites**
1	**teaspoon vanilla**
¼	**teaspoon cream of tartar**
½	**cup sugar**
	Miniature semisweet chocolate pieces

Line 2 large cookie sheets with brown paper or foil (see photo 1). Set aside. In a small mixer bowl beat egg whites, vanilla, and cream of tartar till soft peaks form (tips curl) (see photo 2). Gradually add sugar, beating till stiff peaks form (tips stand straight) (see photo 3).

Put egg white mixture in a decorating bag fitted with a ½-inch round tip, filling bag half full. Squeeze bag gently to form a 1½- to 2-inch circle on the cookie sheet. Make two slightly smaller circles above the first circle, with edges touching, to form a snowman (see photo 4). Repeat with remaining egg white mixture, placing snowmen about 1 inch apart. Place miniature chocolate pieces on smaller top circles for eyes and on larger bottom circles for buttons.

Bake in a 300° oven for 10 to 12 minutes or till cookies just start to turn brown. Turn oven off. Let cookies dry in the oven with the door closed for 30 minutes. Makes about 24.

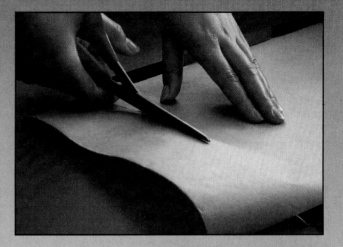

1 Cover two cookie sheets with plain, ungreased brown paper, aluminum foil, or parchment paper. You can purchase brown paper in rolls at the supermarket, or cut up a clean brown-paper bag.

2 Beat the egg whites to soft peaks with an electric mixer on *medium* speed. The egg white foam will be white and, when the beaters are lifted out, the tips of the peaks will bend over, as shown.

3 After soft peaks form, beat on *high* speed till stiff peaks form. The egg whites should look very white and glossy, and peaks should stand straight when the beaters are lifted out, as shown.

4 Pipe the beaten egg white mixture through a decorating bag onto the paper- or foil-lined cookie sheet. Make three circles, each a bit smaller than the previous one.

Meringue Surprises

Buried beneath a snowy layer of meringue hides a chocolate-mint surprise.

3   egg whites
1   teaspoon vanilla
¼   teaspoon cream of tartar
¾   cup sugar
  About 30 layered chocolate-mint wafers, broken in half

Line 2 large cookie sheets with foil (see photo 1, page 102). Grease foil. Set aside. In a large mixer bowl beat egg whites, vanilla, and cream of tartar till soft peaks form (tips curl) (see photo 2, page 103). Gradually add sugar, beating till stiff peaks form (tips stand straight) (see photo 3, page 103).

Drop by rounded tablespoons 1½ inches apart onto prepared cookie sheets (see photo 2, page 31). Press *2* mint wafer halves into *each* cookie. With a knife or narrow spatula, bring meringue up and over candy and swirl the top. Seal meringue around mint well.

Bake in a 300° oven for 20 to 25 minutes or till cookies just start to turn brown. Remove *immediately* and cool completely on wire racks (see photo 4, page 31). Makes about 30.

Peanut Butter-Cocoa Macaroons

Store these chewy cookies overnight in a tightly covered container. For longer storage, keep them in the freezer.

⅓   cup peanut butter
¼   cup sugar
¼   cup unsweetened cocoa powder
3   egg whites
1   teaspoon vanilla
½   cup sugar
1   3½-ounce can (1⅓ cups) flaked coconut
  Cocoa powder (optional)

Grease a cookie sheet. Set aside. In a small heavy saucepan melt peanut butter over low heat, stirring constantly. Set aside to cool. In a small mixing bowl stir together the ¼ cup sugar and cocoa powder. Set aside.

In a large mixer bowl beat egg whites and vanilla till soft peaks form (tips curl) (see photo 2, page 103). Gradually add the ½ cup sugar, beating till stiff peaks form (tips stand straight) (see photo 3, page 103). Fold in the cocoa mixture, peanut butter, and coconut.

Drop by rounded teaspoons 2 inches apart onto prepared cookie sheet (see photo 2, page 31). Bake in a 325° oven about 20 minutes or till set and lightly browned on the edges. Remove and cool completely on wire racks (see photo 4, page 31). Dust with additional cocoa powder, if desired. Makes about 30.

Almond-Orange Macaroons

What do you do with those extra egg yolks? Instead of throwing them out, substitute 2 yolks for 1 whole egg in scrambled eggs, custard, or pudding.

2   **egg whites**
½   **teaspoon vanilla**
⅔   **cup sugar**
¾   **cup flaked coconut**
¼   **cup chopped almonds, toasted**
2   **teaspoons grated orange peel**

Grease a cookie sheet. Set aside. In a small mixer bowl beat egg whites and vanilla till soft peaks form (tips curl) (see photo 2, page 103). Gradually add sugar, beating till stiff peaks form (tips stand straight) (see photo 3, page 103). Fold in coconut, almonds, and orange peel.

Drop by rounded teaspoons 1½ inches apart onto prepared cookie sheet (see photo 2, page 31). Bake in a 325° oven for 10 to 12 minutes or till set and lightly browned on the edges. Remove and cool completely on wire racks (see photo 4, page 31). Makes about 36.

Macaroons

2   **egg whites**
½   **teaspoon vanilla**
⅔   **cup sugar**
1   **cup flaked coconut**
¾   **cup finely chopped macadamia nuts**
     or hazelnuts (filberts)

Grease a cookie sheet. Set aside. In a small mixer bowl beat egg whites and vanilla till soft peaks form (tips curl) (see photo 2, page 103). Gradually add sugar, beating till stiff peaks form (tips stand straight) (see photo 3, page 103). Fold in coconut and nuts.

Drop by rounded tablespoons 2 inches apart onto prepared cookie sheet (see photo 2, page 31). Bake in a 325° oven for 10 to 12 minutes or till set and lightly browned on the edges. Remove and cool completely on wire racks (see photo 4, page 31). Makes about 36.

Beat It!

With a little "eggs-tra" knowledge about eggs, you can turn out perfect meringue and macaroon cookies every time.
● Go ahead and separate cold eggs, but let them stand at room temperature about an hour before beating them.
● Separate the eggs carefully—even the smallest amount of egg yolk can prevent the whites from whipping to peaks.
● Use a straight-sided, nonplastic container for beating egg whites. Plastics can retain fats from previous foods and keep the whites from becoming stiff and fluffy.

● Beating egg whites for just the right amount of time before and after adding the sugar is critical. Before you start adding sugar, beat the egg whites just till soft peaks form (that's when the tips of the egg whites curl—see page 103). If you beat the egg whites too much before the sugar is added, they won't fluff as high and will look curdled. Once you've added the sugar, beat the egg whites just till glossy stiff peaks form (that's when the tips stand straight—see page 103).

Cookie Cones and Curls

Cheers! For celebrations and soirees, gala get-togethers, and festive affairs, these cookie cones and curls are a *must* on your invitation list.

With a little practice, you'll soon become an expert cookie roller. Then, depending on the occasion, you can wrap cookies loosely for cone shapes or tightly for cookie curls.

All it takes is one appearance and these cookies will be the talk of the town.

Almond Snaps

Almond Snaps

What happens if the telephone rings as you're rolling up these cookies? Hang up fast and pop the cookie sheet back into the oven for 30 seconds. This softens the cookies and makes them pliable again.

½ **cup packed brown sugar**
½ **cup butter *or* margarine**
⅓ **cup light corn syrup**
1 **cup ground almonds**
½ **cup all-purpose flour**

Line a cookie sheet with foil (see photo 1, page 102). Grease foil. Set aside. In a small saucepan combine brown sugar, butter or margarine, and corn syrup. Cook and stir over medium heat till butter or margarine is melted and mixture is smooth. Remove from heat. Stir in almonds, flour, and 2 tablespoons *water* (see photo 1).

Drop by rounded measuring teaspoons about 5 inches apart onto prepared cookie sheet (see photo 2). (Bake only 3 or 4 at a time.) Bake in a 350° oven for 6 to 8 minutes or till done.

Let stand on cookie sheet about 2 minutes. *Immediately* remove from cookie sheet, 1 at a time, and roll around a metal cone (see photo 3). Slip cookie off cone. Cool on wire racks (see photo 4, page 31). Makes about 40.

1 Remove the saucepan from the heat. Use a wooden spoon to stir in the ground nuts, flour, and water.

2 Drop rounded measuring teaspoons of the cookie batter onto a greased, foil-lined cookie sheet. The cookies spread a lot as they bake, so leave plenty of room between cookies.

---

3 Quickly roll each warm cookie around a metal cone. (If you don't have a metal cone, make a cone from pliable cardboard.) *Or,* roll the cookies around the greased handle of a wooden spoon. As the cookies cool, they crisp up and hold their shape.

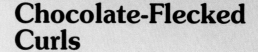

Chocolate-Flecked Curls

2 egg whites
½ teaspoon vanilla
½ cup sugar
½ cup all-purpose flour
1 square (1 ounce) semisweet chocolate, grated
¼ teaspoon ground cinnamon
¼ cup butter *or* margarine, melted and cooled

Line a cookie sheet with foil (see photo 1, page 102). Grease two 4-inch circles on foil. Set aside. Beat egg whites and vanilla till soft peaks form (tips curl) (see photo 2, page 103). Gradually add sugar, beating till stiff peaks form (tips stand straight) (see photo 3, page 103). Combine flour, chocolate, and cinnamon. Gradually beat flour mixture into egg whites at low speed. Stir in butter or margarine till combined.

Drop a small mound of batter (two level measuring teaspoons) onto each greased spot (see photo 2). Spread with the back of a spoon into 3-inch circles. Bake in a 350° oven for 6 to 8 minutes or till done. *Immediately* remove from the cookie sheet and roll around the greased handle of a wooden spoon (see photo 3). Slip cookie off spoon. Cool completely (see photo 4, page 31). Repeat with remaining batter (see note, below). Makes about 30 to 36.

NOTE: You can bake up to 3 two-cookie batches before placing clean foil on the cookie sheet. Grease 2 circles on opposite sides for first batch. For second and third batches, grease areas on cookie sheet that haven't been used.

109

Deep-Fried Cookies

A rose by any other name wouldn't taste nearly as sweet as a Rosette.

Each cookie begins with a batter that's deep-fried to a golden brown. And by simply changing molds, you can use the rosette iron to give your cookie bouquet an assortment of shapes.

As delicate as a tender rosebud, these crisp, light cookies blossom into a grand treat.

Rosettes

Rosettes

1 egg
1 tablespoon sugar
½ cup all-purpose flour
½ cup milk
1 teaspoon vanilla
Cooking oil for deep-fat frying
Powdered sugar

For batter, in a medium mixing bowl stir together egg and sugar. Add flour, milk, and vanilla and beat with a rotary beater till smooth.

Heat a rosette iron in deep hot oil (375°) for 30 seconds (see photo 1). Remove iron from oil and drain on paper towels.

Dip the hot iron into batter (batter should extend three-fourths of the way up side of iron) (see photo 2). Immediately dip iron into hot oil. Fry for 15 to 20 seconds or till golden. Lift iron out of oil, tipping slightly to drain.

Use a fork to push rosette off iron onto paper towels on a wire rack (see photo 3). Repeat with remaining batter, reheating iron about 10 seconds each time. Sift powdered sugar over cooled rosettes (see photo 4). Makes 20 to 25.

1 Dip the rosette iron into the preheated oil. The iron is actually a mold that's mounted on the end of a long steel handle. The long handle lets you dip the mold into the hot oil without fear of burns.

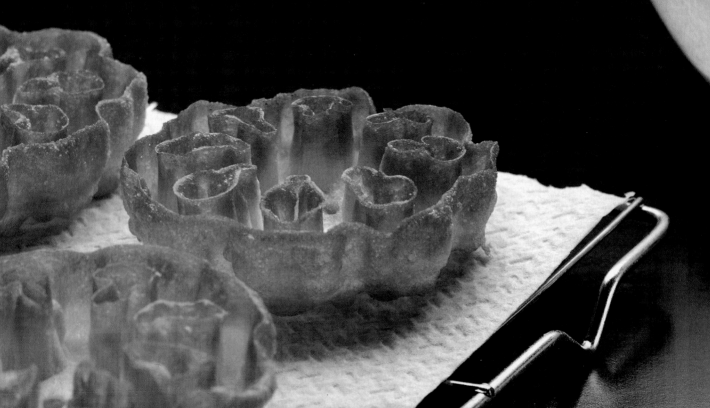

2 Quickly dip the preheated iron into the batter. Be careful not to let the batter go over the top edge or you'll have to break the rosette to get it off of the iron.

3 Use a fork to carefully push the rosette off the iron onto paper towels. Put the paper towels on a wire cooling rack so the rosettes don't become soggy on the bottom as they cool.

4 Continue making rosettes until you've used all the batter. Once all the rosettes have cooled, sift powdered sugar over the tops.

Wild West Main Street

Hankerin' for a cookie, pardner? Meet me on Main Street at high noon for a rootin'-tootin' good cookie.

Relive the golden days of yesteryear with our gingerbread Wild West Main Street. Have a chew on the cobblestone gingerbread street and yummy store fronts. Mosey on down the center of town and find a licorice hitching post, almond thatched stores, and a peppermint barber pole.

Everything in this town is downright delicious. There ain't a wrangler at your ranch who'll turn down this treat.

Wild West Main Street

Wild West Main Street

2½ cups all-purpose flour
1 teaspoon ground ginger
½ teaspoon baking soda
½ teaspoon ground cinnamon
½ cup butter *or* margarine
½ cup sugar
½ cup molasses
White Creamy Frosting
Assorted candies
Sliced almonds

Make a 12×6-inch cardboard or paper pattern for the storefront. Make a 12×4-inch pattern for the road. Set patterns aside.

Grease 2 cookie sheets. Set aside. Combine flour, ginger, soda, and cinnamon (see photo 1, page 14). In a large mixer bowl beat butter with an electric mixer for 30 seconds. Add sugar; beat till fluffy (see photo 1, page 31). Add molasses; beat well. Gradually add flour mixture, beating till combined. Work in the last part of the flour mixture by hand (see photo 1).

Roll dough into a 14x11-inch rectangle directly onto 1 of the prepared cookie sheets. Place floured patterns on dough, leaving a ½-inch space between patterns. Cut around patterns (see photo 2). Cut 4 support triangles from remaining strip of dough. Transfer triangles to the other prepared cookie sheet. Give road a brick appearance by scoring it with a knife. Score lines on storefront to create buildings.

Bake in a 375° oven about 10 minutes or till edges are firm and bottoms are lightly browned (see photo 3, page 43). (Bake triangles for 6 to 8 minutes.) Remove and cool completely on wire racks (see photo 4, page 31).

Decorate storefront with White Creamy Frosting, candies, and almonds (see photo 3). Generously frost the long, straight edges of the triangles and attach to the back of the storefront for support (see photo 4). Attach road to front of building in the same manner. Decorate remaining areas. Makes 1 building, 1 road, and 4 triangles.

White Creamy Frosting: In a large mixer bowl beat ¾ cup *shortening* and ¾ teaspoon *vanilla* for 30 seconds. Gradually beat in 1¾ cups sifted *powdered sugar*. Add 5 teaspoons *milk*. Gradually beat in 1¾ cups sifted *powdered sugar* and enough *milk* to make frosting of piping consistency.

1 The cookie dough will be very stiff, so use a wooden spoon, not your mixer, to stir in the last half of the flour mixture.

2 Roll the dough directly onto the prepared cookie sheet. Place the patterns for the road and the store-front about ½ inch apart. Cut around the patterns with a knife.

3 Decorate the storefront buildings using frosting, assorted candy pieces, and nuts.

4 Generously pipe or spread frosting onto the straight edges of the triangles. To support the storefront, attach the triangles at right angles to the back of the storefront. Attach the road to the front of the building in the same way. Decorate remaining areas with frosting and candies.

Cookie-Baking Hints

Get ready, get set, go bake cookies! But wait a minute—not so fast. When you're investing time, energy, and money into cookie baking, you want guaranteed success. Simply follow our easy-to-read recipes and these simple pointers, and your cookie baking will run smoothly each and every time.

Successful Cookie Baking

● Read the entire recipe before you start, then follow all of the directions exactly.

● Check to see that you have all of the ingredients and equipment on hand. Always use the finest quality, freshest ingredients available. Once you're familiar with a recipe, you can vary the spices and personalize it to suit your tastes. But remember that even a slight change in a key ingredient can significantly alter the end result.

● Measure all of the ingredients accurately. Use liquid measuring cups for liquids and graduated measuring cups for dry ingredients.

● Beat butter or margarine with an electric mixer on *medium* speed about

30 seconds to soften it. Using high speed may sling the butter or margarine out of the bowl, and low speed isn't powerful enough to cream the butter or margarine as much as desired.
- Preheat the oven about 10 minutes before baking any cookies.
- Always place cookie dough on cool cookie sheets to keep the dough from spreading.
- Bake on the middle oven rack for even baking and browning.

- Check cookies for doneness at the minimum baking time given in each recipe. Use a timer to avoid guesswork.

Storing Cookies
- To protect cookies from air and humidity that can make them stale, keep cooled cookies in tightly covered containers. Store bar cookies this

way or in their baking pan, tightly covered with plastic wrap or foil.
- Remember not to store soft and crisp cookies in the same container, or the crisp ones will soon be soft.
- To restore moisture to soft cookies that have begun to dry out, place a wedge of raw apple or a slice of bread on a piece of waxed paper. Put it right into the container with the cookies and seal tightly. Remove the apple or bread after 24 hours.

- For long-term storage, freeze baked cookies in freezer containers or plastic bags for up to a year. Before serving, thaw the cookies right in the containers or the plastic bags.
- Bulk dough, except for meringue-type dough, can be frozen for baking later. Store the dough in freezer containers for up to 6 months. Before baking, thaw it in the freezer containers.

Giving Cookie Gifts

Baking cookies is twice the fun when you share the results with someone. Whether it's a special occasion like Christmas or a care package to a hungry student, an array of home-baked cookies brightens the day for both of you—unless the cookies arrive as crumbs! Read on and heed these suggestions for packing cookies cleverly and for mailing them successfully.

The Right Container
Half the fun of giving cookie gifts is searching for that perfect container—one that fits your budget, suits the goody, and will be kept long after the last cookie crumb is gone.

Containers can be as plain or as fancy as you want to make them. Ribbon-tied paper sacks or gussied-up coffee cans or shortening cans are some of the simplest homemade carriers for cookies. Gift shops stock many clever cardboard containers printed with bright graphics. These make delightful and often reusable gift packages. And don't overlook the ever-popular cookie tin.

Whatever the outside container, be sure the cookies inside are well protected from air and moisture. Even the most attractively packaged cookies will be a disappointment if they're stale. When the container you're using doesn't have a tight-fitting lid, wrap the cookies in plastic wrap or seal them in a plastic bag before placing them in the container.

Mailing Cookie Gifts

Choose cookies that travel well. Most bar cookies are good senders, as are soft, moist, drop cookies. Frosted and filled cookies aren't good choices because the frosting or filling may soften, causing the cookies to stick to each other or to the wrapping. If you want to send cutout cookies, send ones with rounded edges instead of points that break off easily.

Perfect Packing

Find a heavy box for sending cookies and line it with plastic wrap or foil. Lay down a generous layer of filler, such as bubble wrap, foam packing pieces, crumpled tissue paper, waxed paper, or brown paper bags.

Wrap cookies in pairs, back to back, or individually with plastic wrap. Using the sturdiest cookies on the bottom, place a single layer of wrapped cookies on top of the base filler. Top with another layer of filler. Continue layering, ending with plenty of filler. The box should be full enough to prevent shifting of its contents when closed.

Wrap It Up

Before closing the box of cookies, insert a card with the addresses of both the sender and the receiver in case the box is accidentally torn open. Use strapping tape to secure the box. (Cellophane and masking tapes may crack, tear, or pull away from the package with exposure to cold or moisture.) Avoid using paper overwraps and string, which may be torn off or caught in automatic equipment.

Address the box and apply transparent tape over the address to keep it from becoming smeared or blurred from moisture or handling. And mark the box "perishable" to encourage careful handling.

Nutrition Analysis Chart

Use these analyses to compare nutritional values of different recipes. This information was calculated using Agriculture Handbook Number 8, published by the United States Department of Agriculture, as the primary source.

In compiling the nutrition analyses, we made the following assumptions:
● Optional ingredients were not included in the nutrition analyses.

● When two ingredient options appear in a recipe, calculations were made using the first one.
● For recipes with a serving range ("Makes 40 to 50 cookies"), calculations were made using the first figure.
● Nutrition analysis figures are based on one cookie per serving.

	Per Serving						Percent U.S. RDA Per Serving							
	Calories	Protein (g)	Carbohydrate (g)	Fat (g)	Sodium (mg)	Potassium (mg)	Protein	Vitamin A	Vitamin C	Thiamine	Riboflavin	Niacin	Calcium	Iron
Bar Cookies														
Apricot Bars (p. 22)	80	1	13	3	40	90	0	8	0	2	2	2	0	4
Butterscotch Blonde Brownies (p. 18)	140	1	21	6	60	75	2	2	0	4	2	0	2	4
Carrot Bars (p. 17)	110	1	13	6	35	40	0	20	0	2	0	0	0	0
Chewy Ginger Bars (p. 16)	110	1	19	3	55	85	0	2	0	2	2	2	2	6
Chocolate-Pecan Bars (p. 24)	150	2	18	8	60	50	2	4	0	4	2	2	0	4
Chocolate Syrup Brownies (p. 17)	180	2	25	8	75	85	2	4	0	2	2	0	0	4
Citrus-Yogurt Squares (p. 14)	150	2	26	4	80	30	2	2	0	4	2	2	2	2
Cocoa Cake Brownies (p. 18)	190	2	24	10	110	65	2	4	0	4	4	2	2	4
Coffee 'n' Cream Bars (p. 26)	110	2	16	5	35	30	2	2	0	2	2	0	0	2
Luscious Lemon Diamonds (p. 24)	120	2	19	4	55	30	2	2	4	2	2	0	0	2
Maple-Pecan Bars (p. 16)	100	1	12	6	40	35	0	2	0	4	2	0	0	2
Mocha Cheesecake Bars (p. 26)	100	2	10	7	65	35	2	4	0	0	2	0	0	2
Orange-Raisin Bars (p. 25)	120	2	17	6	60	70	2	2	2	4	2	2	2	2
Peanut-Oat Bars (p. 25)	130	3	13	8	65	85	4	2	0	2	2	4	0	2
Cookie Mix Cookies														
Banana Chippers (p. 55)	80	1	10	4	10	30	0	0	0	2	0	0	0	2
Carrot Cookies (p. 55)	70	1	9	3	10	35	0	20	0	2	2	0	0	2
Cranberry Drops (p. 54)	60	1	8	4	10	25	0	0	0	2	0	0	0	0
Great Cocoa Bars (p. 53)	139	2	15	7	29	55	2	0	0	2	2	0	0	2
Gumdrop Cookies (p. 50)	100	1	13	5	15	20	0	0	0	2	2	0	0	2
Jam Gems (p. 55)	90	1	10	6	10	35	2	0	0	2	2	0	0	2
Make-a-Cookie Mix (p. 50)	710	6	93	36	80	150	8	0	0	25	15	15	8	20
Oatmeal-Peanut Cookies (p. 54)	80	2	9	4	25	50	2	0	0	2	0	2	0	2
Raisin Bars (p. 53)	100	1	15	4	20	50	0	0	0	2	0	0	0	2
Cookie Tarts														
Bonbon Bites (p. 67)	90	1	10	5	45	20	0	2	0	2	0	0	0	0
Fruited Sesame Tassies (p. 66)	70	1	12	3	25	55	0	2	0	2	0	0	0	2
Fudgy Liqueur Cups (p. 67)	110	1	12	6	75	25	2	4	0	0	2	0	0	2
Mini Cheesecake Tarts (p. 64)	100	2	9	7	70	25	2	4	0	2	2	0	0	2
Rocky Road Tarts (p. 66)	140	2	12	10	60	60	2	4	0	2	4	0	2	2

	Calories	Protein (g)	Carbohydrate (g)	Fat (g)	Sodium (mg)	Potassium (mg)	Protein	Vitamin A	Vitamin C	Thiamine	Riboflavin	Niacin	Calcium	Iron
Cutout Cookies														
Butterscotch-Stuffed Cocoa Cookies (p. 87)	60	1	8	3	35	10	0	0	0	0	0	0	0	0
Chocolate Cutouts (p. 72)	45	1	6	2	20	20	0	0	0	0	0	0	0	0
Cinnamon Shortbread (p. 72)	100	1	10	6	60	10	0	4	0	4	2	2	0	2
Cocoa Shortbread (p. 72)	100	1	10	6	65	15	0	4	0	4	2	2	0	2
Decorated Sugar Cookies (p. 75)	80	1	14	2	20	10	0	0	0	0	0	0	0	0
Fruity Pillows (p. 86)	120	1	18	5	30	30	0	0	0	4	2	2	0	2
German Honey Cakes (p. 74)	150	2	33	1	35	120	2	0	0	6	4	4	2	6
Gingerbread Gems (p. 87)	90	1	12	4	35	45	2	0	0	4	2	2	0	4
Gingerbread People (p. 75)	70	1	12	2	20	40	0	0	0	2	0	0	0	2
High-in-the-Sky Cookie Pops (p. 70)	90	2	17	3	60	20	2	0	0	4	2	2	0	2
Orange-Ginger Shortbread (p. 72)	100	1	10	6	60	10	0	4	0	4	2	2	0	2
Overstuffed Pockets (p. 86)	90	1	12	5	5	30	0	2	0	4	2	2	0	2
Scottish Shortbread (p. 72)	100	1	10	6	60	10	0	4	0	4	2	2	0	2
Spicy Cream Cheese Cookies (p. 74)	110	2	16	4	75	30	2	2	0	4	2	2	0	4
Sugar and Spice Rounds (p. 84)	140	2	18	7	80	60	2	4	0	4	2	2	0	2
Whole Wheat Joe Froggers (p. 72)	220	3	37	7	110	230	4	4	0	10	6	6	6	10
Wild West Main Street (p. 116)	250	2	35	11	70	100	2	2	0	6	4	4	2	6
Drop Cookies														
Apple Pie Cookies (p. 33)	70	1	12	3	40	15	0	2	0	2	0	0	0	2
Coconut-Almond Marvels (p. 33)	120	2	14	8	20	95	2	0	0	0	2	0	0	4
Double-Chocolate Chunk Specials (p. 32)	90	1	12	5	45	40	0	0	0	2	2	0	0	2
Double-Wheat Chippers (p. 30)	110	1	13	7	50	65	2	2	0	2	2	2	0	2
Hazelnut-Mocha Marvels (p. 33)	130	2	13	9	15	100	2	0	0	2	0	0	2	4
Oatmeal Chippers (p. 30)	110	1	13	7	40	55	2	0	0	2	0	0	0	2
Oatmeal Wheat Treats (p. 32)	70	1	8	4	25	30	0	0	0	2	0	0	0	0
Old-Fashioned Chocolate Chippers (p. 30)	110	1	13	7	40	50	0	0	0	2	2	0	0	2
Rough and Ready Ranger Cookies (p. 47)	60	1	8	3	40	30	0	0	0	2	0	2	0	2
Sour Cream Apricot Drops (p. 35)	100	1	16	4	45	85	0	8	0	2	0	0	0	2
Hand-Shaped Cookies														
Chocolate-Topped Almond Fingers (p. 47)	80	1	11	4	35	20	0	2	0	2	2	0	0	0
Cinnamon Candy Cane Cookies (p. 60)	70	1	8	4	25	10	0	0	0	2	0	0	0	0
Citrus Kringla (p. 60)	80	1	12	3	75	20	2	0	0	4	2	2	2	2
Decorated Berliner Kranzer (p. 61)	90	1	9	6	55	10	0	4	0	2	2	2	0	2
Flaky Dutch Letters (p. 61)	360	6	26	26	200	135	8	15	0	10	10	8	4	8
Honey 'n' Spice Cookies (p. 44)	70	1	10	3	25	10	0	0	0	2	0	0	0	0
Molasses-Spice Cookies (p. 46)	70	1	10	3	50	40	0	0	0	2	0	0	0	2
Old-Fashioned Sandies (p. 46)	80	1	7	6	40	20	0	2	0	4	0	0	0	2
Peanut Butter Critters (p. 42)	170	3	18	9	110	75	4	2	0	4	2	6	0	2
Peppered Pfeffernuesse (p. 47)	50	1	9	2	30	45	0	0	0	2	2	2	0	2
Praline Sandies (p. 46)	80	1	7	6	40	20	0	2	0	4	0	0	0	2
Spicy Wheat Wreaths (p. 58)	120	1	15	6	65	20	2	4	0	4	2	2	0	2
Whole Wheat-Peanut Butter Blossoms (p. 44)	90	2	11	5	30	60	2	0	0	2	2	2	2	2

	Per Serving					Percent U.S. RDA Per Serving							
	Calories	Protein (g)	Carbohydrate (g)	Fat (g)	Sodium (mg)	Potassium (mg)	Protein	Vitamin A	Vitamin C	Thiamine	Riboflavin	Niacin	Calcium	Iron
Meringues and Macaroons														
Almond-Orange Macaroons (p. 105)	30	0	5	1	5	15	0	0	0	0	0	0	0	0
Macaroons (p. 105)	45	0	5	3	10	20	0	0	0	0	0	0	0	0
Meringue Snowmen (p. 102)	25	0	5	1	0	10	0	0	0	0	0	0	0	0
Meringue Surprises (p. 104)	60	1	11	1	15	15	0	0	0	0	0	0	0	0
Peanut Butter-Cocoa Macaroons (p. 104)	60	1	7	3	30	40	2	0	0	0	0	2	0	0
Miscellaneous														
Almond Snaps (p. 108)	60	1	6	3	25	25	0	0	0	0	0	0	0	0
Ambrosia Cookie Pizza (p. 38)	200	3	26	10	90	65	4	6	0	6	4	2	2	4
Big Chipper Cookiewich (p. 39)	210	2	25	12	75	75	2	4	0	4	2	2	2	6
Chocolate-Flecked Curls (p. 109)	40	0	5	2	20	10	0	0	0	0	0	0	0	0
Rosettes (p. 112)	30	1	3	1	5	15	0	0	0	0	0	0	0	0
No-Bake Cookies														
Chocolate Rum Balls (p. 10)	45	1	9	1	10	65	0	6	0	0	0	0	0	2
Choco-Peanut Squares (p. 8)	100	2	12	5	65	65	2	2	2	2	2	6	0	2
Cinnamon-Marshmallow Squares (p. 10)	120	1	23	3	140	40	0	10	6	8	8	8	0	4
Crisp Peanut Balls (p. 8)	45	1	5	2	35	30	0	0	0	0	0	4	0	0
Rocky Road Drops (p. 10)	90	1	10	6	15	65	2	0	0	2	2	4	0	4
Tropical Fruit Balls (p. 10)	35	1	6	1	10	35	0	0	0	0	0	0	0	0
Pressed Cookies														
Coconut-Cocoa Spritz (p. 99)	70	1	8	4	10	10	0	2	0	2	0	0	0	0
Double-Peanut Spritz (p. 96)	70	2	7	4	30	55	2	0	0	0	2	0	0	0
Nutty Spritz (p. 98)	70	1	8	4	40	20	0	2	0	2	0	0	0	0
Pressed Gingerbread Cookies (p. 99)	80	1	10	4	45	35	0	2	0	2	2	2	0	2
Spritz (p. 98)	80	1	9	5	55	10	0	2	0	2	0	0	0	0
Sliced Cookies														
Apricot-Nut Swirls (p. 92)	70	1	10	3	45	45	0	4	0	2	0	0	0	2
Buttery Almond Slices (p. 80)	70	1	8	4	35	25	0	2	0	2	2	0	0	0
Cardamom-Lemon Refrigerator Cookies (p. 81)	70	1	8	4	25	15	0	0	0	2	0	0	0	0
Choco-Peanut Butter Cookie Roll (p. 93)	80	1	9	4	40	45	2	0	0	0	0	2	0	2
Cranberry-Orange Twirls (p. 92)	70	1	9	3	45	10	0	2	0	2	0	0	0	0
Grasshopper Cookie Sandwiches (p. 78)	110	1	16	5	45	10	0	2	0	2	0	0	0	0
Molasses-Date Sliced Cookies (p. 81)	60	1	10	2	5	50	0	0	0	2	0	0	0	2
Pistachio Pinwheels (p. 90)	70	1	8	4	20	35	0	0	0	2	0	0	0	0
Whole Wheat-Peanut Slices (p. 80)	80	2	9	5	30	40	2	0	0	2	0	2	0	2

Have BETTER HOMES AND
GARDENS® magazine
delivered to your door. For
information, write to:
MR. ROBERT AUSTIN
P.O. BOX 4536
DES MOINES, IA 50336